Polish Your Furniture

With Panty Hose

Also by Joey Green

Hellbent on Insanity

The Unofficial Gilligan's Island Handbook

The Get Smart Handbook

The Partridge Family Album

Polish Your Furniture With Panty Hose

AND HUNDREDS OF OFFBEAT USES FOR BRAND-NAME PRODUCTS

Joey Green

HYPERION

New York

The author has compiled the information contained herein from a variety of sources, and neither the author nor the distributors can assume responsibility for the effectiveness of the suggestions. Caution is urged in the use of the cleaning solutions, folk medicine remedies, and pest control substances. Many of the products pictured and mentioned in this book are registered trademarks. The companies that own these trademarks do not endorse all of the suggestions in this book. Specifically, The Coca-Cola Company does not endorse any use of Coca-Cola other than as a soft drink. Procter & Gamble does not recommend or endorse any use of Bounce, Ivory soap, Jif, Dawn, or Pampers beyond those for which these products have been tested as indicated on the usage instructions on each package label. For a full listing of trademarks, see page 139.

All photographs herein are reprinted by permission of the trademark holders.

Design by Joey Green

Library of Congress Cataloging-in-Publication Data

Green, Joey.
    Polish your furniture with panty hose : and hundreds of offbeat uses for brand-name products / Joey Green.
      p.   cm.
    Includes bibliographical references and index.
    ISBN 0-7868-8108-9
    1. Home economics. 2. Brand name products—United States. 3. Medicine, Popular. I. Title
TX158.G68 1996   95–16399
640′.41—dc20   CIP

First Edition
10 9 8 7 6 5 4 3 2 1

For Elaine and Harry

Ingredients

But First, A Word From Our Sponsor

When I was an advertising copywriter at J. Walter Thompson in New York, I was invited to attend a very strange brainstorming session. Eight of us from different departments in the agency were gathered together in a conference room and asked to generate a list of alternative uses for Nestea Iced Tea Mix that could be advertised to increase sales. Until that meeting, I had no idea that bathing in Nestea soothed sunburn pain. Nestea never advertised that fact—unless, of course, that was the subliminal message in "Take the Nestea Plunge."

That meeting changed my life forever. While I've never bathed in Nestea, I realized that there are hundreds of alternative uses for well-known products kept secret from the American public. I was determined to unearth this cache of withheld information. So I quit my job and spent the next ten years on a quest to uncover the hundreds of mysterious uses for products like Coca-Cola, Vaseline, and WD-40.

I learned some startling truths. Jif peanut butter doubles as axle grease. Efferdent cleans diamonds. SPAM luncheon meat works as furniture polish. But a slew of unanswered questions preyed on my conscience. How did Worcestershire Sauce get its name? Who developed Silly Putty? How was the Ziploc Storage Bag invented? And, above all, is America ready to know?

This book is the culmination of my obsessive journey into the bowels of American know-how. I hope you'll agree it was well worth the trip.

Bounce

■ **Repel mosquitoes.** Tie a sheet of Bounce through a belt loop when outdoors during mosquito season.

■ **Eliminate static electricity from your television screen.** Since Bounce is designed to help eliminate static cling, wipe your television screen with a used sheet of Bounce to help prevent dust from resettling.

■ **Dissolve soap scum from shower doors.** Clean with a used sheet of Bounce.

■ **Freshen the air in your home.** Place an individual sheet of Bounce in a drawer or hang one in the closet.

■ **Prevent thread from tangling.** Run a threaded needle through a sheet of Bounce to eliminate the static cling on the thread before sewing.

■ **Eliminate static cling from panty hose.** Rub a damp, used sheet of Bounce over the hose.

■ **Prevent musty suitcases.** Place an individual sheet of Bounce inside empty luggage before storing.

■ **Freshen the air in your car.** Place a sheet of Bounce under the front seat.

■ **Clean baked-on food from a cooking pan.** Put a sheet in the pan, fill with water, let sit overnight, and sponge clean. The antistatic agents apparently weaken the bond between the food and the pan while the fabric softening agents soften the baked-on food.

■ **Eliminate odors in wastebaskets.** Place a sheet of Bounce at the bottom of the wastebasket.

■ **Collect cat hair.** Rubbing the area with a sheet of Bounce will magnetically attract all the loose hairs.

■ **Eliminate static electricity from venetian blinds.** Wipe the blinds with a used sheet of Bounce to prevent dust from resettling.

■ **Wipe up sawdust from drilling or sandpapering.** A used sheet of Bounce will collect sawdust like a tack cloth.

■ **Eliminate odors in dirty laundry.** Place an individual sheet of Bounce at the bottom of a laundry bag or hamper.

■ **Deodorize shoes or sneakers.** Place a sheet of Bounce

in your shoes or sneakers overnight so they'll smell great in the morning.

Invented
1972

The Name
The name Bounce signifies the way the sheet of fabric softener tumbles with the load during a typical drying cycle, distributing its softening ingredients.

A Short History
When different dry fabrics rub together in the dryer, the electrons in one fabric transfer to another, creating static electricity. When one fabric has more electrons than another, the fabrics cling together. To prevent static cling, Procter & Gamble developed Bounce to act as a conductor, releasing molecules of fabric softener that give the fabrics similar surface characteristics, preventing electron transfer.

Ingredients
Fabric softening agents (cationic and/or nonionic surfactants), an antistatic agent (hydrophilic polymer or nonionic surfactant), an agent to provide more uniform ingredient release (bentonite), in a non-woven cloth

Strange Facts

■ The actual sheet is nine inches square and made from non-woven porous rayon cloth.

■ Bounce reduces the amount of effort needed during ironing because its softening agents act to smooth fibers, reduce wrinkles, and help the iron glide more easily.

Distribution

■ Bounce fabric softener sheets can be found in more than one out of every four homes in the United States. (Fabric softener can be found in 85 percent of all homes in the United States; 78 percent of those homes use Bounce.)

■ Bounce is available in Outdoor Fresh Bounce, Gentle Breeze Bounce, and Bounce Free (with no fragrance).

For More Information

Procter & Gamble, Co., 391 East 6th Street, Cincinnati, OH 45202. Or telephone 1-800-5-BOUNCE.

Clairol

Herbal Essences

■ **Remove ring-around-the-collar.** Since the dirt rings in collars are oil stains, oily hair shampoo will remove them when rubbed into the fabric.

■ **Wash dishes.** If you run out of dishwashing soap, wash your dishes in the kitchen sink with Herbal Essences. It's perfect for camping because it's biodegradable.

■ **Make a bubble bath.** Pour one capful of Herbal Essences under a running tap in the bathtub.

■ **Clean grease from your hands.** A dab of Herbal Essences cuts through the grime on your hands.

■ **Wash your car.** Add two capfuls of Herbal Essences to a bucket of water and soap up your car with the biodegradable suds.

■ **Clean hairbrushes and combs.** Add a capful of Herbal Essences to warm water. Shampoo cuts through sebum oil, leaving brushes clean and fresh.

■ **Shave.** Apply Herbal Essences to wet skin as a substitute for shaving cream.

Invented
1971

The Name
Clairol is apparently a combination of the French word *clair* (clear) and the suffix *-ol* (oil). Herbal Essence, the name of the original green shampoo, referred to the shampoo's herbal fragrance, not its ingredients. In 1995, Clairol reformulated the shampoo with all-natural ingredients and renamed it Herbal Essences.

A Short History
The scalp releases sebum oil into the hair, which in turn causes dirt to stick to the hair. In the 1890s, German chemists discovered the detergents that would wash sebum oil from hair, although British hairdressers had already coined the word *shampoo* from the Hindi *champoo* (to massage) to refer to cleansing formulas made from water, soap, and soda. In the United States, John Breck, captain of a Massachusetts volunteer fire department, developed several shampoos—including a shampoo for normal hair in 1930 and shampoos for oily and dry hair in 1933. Clairol concocted green Herbal Es-

sence shampoo to target the back-to-nature sentiment embraced by the youth movement of the early 1970s. In 1995, Clairol reformulated, repackaged, and relaunched Herbal Essence as a complete line of biodegradable shampoos blended from organic herbs and botanicals in pure mountain springwater, renaming the product Herbal Essences.

Ingredients

Water, sodium laureth sulfate, sodium lauryl sulfate, cocamidopropyl betaine, aloe extract, chamomile extract, passion flower extract, cocamide MEA, dihydroxypropyl PEG-5 linoleaminium chloride, fragrance, citric acid, propylene glycol, DMDM hydantoin, iodopropynyl butylcarbamate, D&C Orange no. 4, Ext. D&C violet no. 2, FD&C yellow no. 5

Strange Facts

■ Biodegradable Herbal Essences is made from natural herbs and botanicals and plant-derived ingredients from renewable plant sources. The herbs and botanicals are grown under certified organic conditions without petrochemicals or pesticides.

■ Herbal Essences is not tested on animals, nor does it contain any animal by-products.

■ The see-through bottles, featuring botanical graphics and a flip-top cap, are made from recyclable polyethylene and contain 25 percent postconsumer polyethylene plastic.

■ Herbal Essences financially supports environmental and natural causes devoted to preserving the earth's rain forests, parks, and endangered plant species.

Distribution

■ Herbal Essences is available in four clear formulas: Moisture-Balancing Shampoo (chamomile, aloe vera, and passion flower), Replenisher Shampoo (rose hips, vitamin E, and jojoba), Extra Body Shampoo (marigold flowers, angelica, and thyme), and Clarifying Shampoo (rosemary, jasmine, and orange flower).

For More Information

Clairol Inc., Stamford, CT 06902. Or telephone 1-800-223-5800.

Coca-Cola

■ **Clean a toilet bowl.** Pour a can of Coca-Cola into the toilet bowl. Let the Real Thing sit for one hour, then brush and flush clean. The citric acid in Coke removes stains from vitreous china, according to household-hints columnist Heloise.

■ **Remove rust spots from chrome car bumpers.** Rubbing the bumper with a crumpled-up piece of Reynolds Wrap aluminum foil dipped in Coca-Cola will help remove rust spots, according to household-hints columnist Mary Ellen.

■ **Clean corrosion from car battery terminals.** Pour a can of carbonated Coca-Cola over the terminals to bubble away the corrosion, according to Heloise.

■ **Cook with Coca-Cola.** The Coca-Cola Consumer Information Center offers a free packet of recipes, including a

Mustard Herb Dressing (an Italian-style salad dressing made with one-half cup Coca-Cola), a Twin Cheese Dip (requiring three-quarters cup Coca-Cola and doubling as a sandwich filling), and Sweet-Sour Cabbage (using one-half cup Coca-Cola and two tablespoons bacon drippings).

■ **Loosen a rusted bolt.** Mary Ellen suggests applying a cloth soaked in a carbonated soda to the rusted bolt for several minutes.

■ **Bake a moist ham.** Empty a can of Coca-Cola into the baking pan, wrap the ham in aluminum foil, and bake. Thirty minutes before the ham is finished, remove the foil, allowing the drippings to mix with the Coke for a sumptuous brown gravy.

■ **Remove grease from clothes.** Empty a can of Coke into a load of greasy work clothes, add detergent, and run through a regular wash cycle. The Coca-Cola will help loosen grease stains, according to Mary Ellen.

Invented
May 8, 1886

The Name
Bookkeeper Frank M. Robinson, one of Coca-Cola inventor Dr. John Styth Pemberton's four partners, suggested naming the elixir after two of the main ingredients: the coca leaf and the kola nut. He suggested spelling *kola* with a *c* for the sake of alliteration. Robinson wrote the name in his bookkeeper's Spencerian script, much the way it appears today.

A Short History

Dr. John Styth Pemberton, inventor of Globe of Flower Cough Syrup, Indian Queen Hair Dye, Triplex Liver Pills, and Extract of Styllinger, was eager to duplicate Vin Mariani, a popular wine elixir made with coca. In his backyard at 107 Marietta Street in Atlanta, Georgia, Pemberton developed a thick syrup drink from sugar water, a kola nut extract, and coca.

Pemberton brought his new syrup elixir to Jacob's Drug Store, where druggist Willis Venable added carbonated water. The rights to the name and formula were bought and sold several times before Asa G. Candler acquired them in 1888. Candler kept the formula a well-guarded secret, and on January 31, 1893, trademarked the name. The distinctively shaped Coke bottle was designed by Alexander Samuelson at Root Glass in Terre Haute, Indiana.

Since 1893, the recipe for Coca-Cola has been changed only once. In 1985, when Pepsi-Cola outsold Coca-Cola in the United States for the first time in history, the Coca-Cola Company sweetened the product and renamed it New Coke. Within three months, consumers forced the company to bring back the old formula. It became known as Coca-Cola Classic, and New Coke, considered the marketing fiasco of the decade, soon disappeared from the marketplace.

Ingredients

Carbonated water, high fructose corn syrup and/or sucrose, caffeine, phosphoric acid, caramel color, glycerin, lemon oil, orange oil, lime oil, cassia oil, nutmeg oil, vanilla extract, coca, and kola

Strange Facts

■ Coca-Cola stock went public in 1919 at $40 per share. In 1994, one of those shares was worth $118,192.76, including dividends.

■ Rumor contends that a piece of meat left in a glass of Coca-Cola overnight will be completely dissolved by the following morning. It won't. A piece of meat soaked in Coca-Cola overnight will, however, be marinated and tender.

■ During the 1960s, the Coca-Cola jingle was sung by Roy Orbison, the Supremes, the Moody Blues, Ray Charles (who sang the Diet Pepsi jingle in the 1990s), the Fifth Dimension, Aretha Franklin, and Gladys Knight and the Pips.

■ The World of Coca-Cola, a three-story pavilion in Atlanta, features exhibits (including a 1,000-piece memorabilia collection and John Pemberton's original handwritten formula book), soda fountains of the past and future, bottling exhibits, samples of Coca-Cola products from around the world, and films of Coca-Cola commercials.

■ If all the Coca-Cola ever produced was in regular-size bottles and laid end to end, it would reach to the moon and back 1,045 times. That is one trip per day for two years, ten months, and eleven days.

■ "Good to the Last Drop," a slogan used by Maxwell House coffee, was first used by Coca-Cola in 1908.

■ Shaking up a bottle of Coca-Cola for use as a douche immediately after sexual intercourse has been considered an effective method of contraception among the uneducated. It does not work.

■ *The Coca-Cola Catalog*, a mail order catalog filled with Coca-Cola memorabilia from boxer shorts to "O" gauge boxcars emblazoned with the Coca-Cola logo, is available for free by calling 1-800-872-6531.

Distribution

■ On the average day in 1993, consumers drank 705 million servings of Coke and other Coca-Cola soft drinks worldwide.

■ 2,386.7 million gallons of Coca-Cola Classic were sold in 1992.

■ Coca-Cola outsells Pepsi worldwide by a more than two-to-one margin.

■ Coca-Cola is available in Coca-Cola Classic, Caffeine Free Coca-Cola Classic, Diet Coke, Caffeine Free Diet Coke, Cherry Coke, Diet Cherry Coke, and Coke II (previously known as New Coke).

For More Information

Consumer Information Center, Coca-Cola USA, One Coca-Cola Plaza, Atlanta, GA 30313. Or telephone 1-800-GET COKE.

Colgate

■ **Polish silverware, silver, or gold.** Colgate will shine up silver and gold. Rinse thoroughly.

■ **Clean piano keys.** Squeeze Colgate on a damp cloth. Rub the keys well, wipe dry, and buff with a soft, dry cloth. After all, ivory comes from an elephant's tusk.

■ **Remove ink spots from cloth.** Squeeze Colgate on spot, scrub, and rinse thoroughly.

■ **Dry up acne pimples.** Dab Colgate on pimples.

■ **Remove crayon from walls.** Brush the marks with Colgate on an old toothbrush.

■ **Remove scratches on glassware.** Polish with a dollop of Colgate.

■ **Deodorize smelly hands.** Squeeze an inch of Colgate into your palm and wash hands under running water.

■ **Remove Kool-Aid mustaches from kids' faces.** Rub on Colgate and rinse thoroughly.

■ **Deodorize "sour" baby bottles.** Scrub with Colgate and a bottle brush.

■ **Remove scuffs on shoes.** Apply Colgate with a tissue, rub, and wipe off.

■ **Remove tar from skin.** Squeeze on Colgate and rub.

■ **Fill small holes in walls.** Use a small dab of Colgate as emergency spackling to fill in small holes in plaster walls. Let dry before painting.

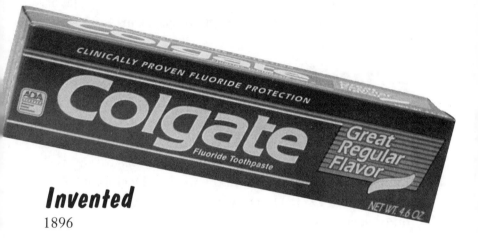

Invented
1896

The Name
The Colgate Company named the white toothpaste after the company's founder, William Colgate.

A Short History
In 1806, William Colgate founded his starch, soap, and candle business on Dutch Street in New York City. In 1896, the Colgate Company, run by Colgate's son, Samuel Colgate, introduced Colgate Dental Cream, the first toothpaste pack-

aged in a collapsible tube. In 1968, Colgate toothpaste was reformulated with MFP fluoride (monofluorophosphate), deemed the best possible protection against tooth decay.

Ingredients

Sodium monofluorophosphate (0.15 percent w/v fluoride ion), dicalcium phosphate dihydrate, water, glycerin and/or sorbitol, sodium lauryl sulfate, cellulose gum, flavor, tetrasodium pyrophosphate, sodium saccharin

Strange Facts

■ Poison toothpaste is used by the CIA as a weapon for assassinations, according to Larry Devlin, a CIA agent who was instructed to kill ousted Belgian Congo prime minister Patrice Lumumba. "I received instructions to see that Lumumba was removed from the world," Devlin told *Time* magazine in 1993. "I received poison toothpaste, among other devices, but never used them."

■ When wilderness camping, anything that smells like food can attract bears, including toothpaste. Food, soap, and toothpaste should be stored in a waterproof sack hung over a twenty-foot-high rope strung between two trees.

■ According to *The First Really Important Survey of American Habits* by Mel Poretz and Barry Sinrod, 72 percent of Americans squeeze the toothpaste tube from the top.

Distribution

■ Colgate is the best-selling toothpaste worldwide.

■ Colgate is available in Great Regular Flavor, Tartar Control Paste, Clear Blue Winterfresh Gel, Tartar Control Gel, Baking Soda, Tartar Control Baking Soda, and Platinum.

For More Information

Colgate-Palmolive Company, 300 Park Avenue, New York, NY 10022. Or telephone 1-800-221-4607.

Dannon Yogurt

■ **Soothe sunburn pain.** Spread yogurt on the sunburn, let sit for twenty minutes, then rinse clean with lukewarm water.

■ **Reduce the occurrence of yeast infections.** The March 1992 issue of the *Annals of Internal Medicine* reports that daily consumption of yogurt containing *Lactobacillus acidophilus* cultures results in a threefold decrease in the incidence of candidal vaginitis (yeast infections).

■ **Enhance your immune system.** According to the *International Journal of Immunotherapy*, yogurt with active cultures enhances the body's immune system by increasing the production of gamma interferons, which play a key role in fighting certain allergies and viral infections. Other studies indicate that yogurt can help prevent gastrointestinal infections. (Lactic acid helps inhibit the growth of food-borne pathogens, and yogurt cultures produce bacteriocins that restore natural intestinal cultures.)

■ **Prevent diarrhea while taking antibiotics.** Eat Dannon Yogurt with active cultures while taking antibiotics. Antibiotics may kill healthful bacteria in addition to disease-bearing ones, but the *Lactobacillus acidophilus* in yogurt produces bacteriocins.

■ **Tighten pores and cleanse skin.** Spread Dannon

Yogurt over your face, wait twenty minutes, then wash with lukewarm water.

■ **Cure yeast infections.** Use a turkey baster to insert yogurt into the vagina. According to *The New Our Bodies, Ourselves*, some women claim that yogurt in the vagina is a remedy for *candida albicans*.

■ **Soothe canker sores.** Eat two servings of Dannon Yogurt a day until the sores clear.

■ **Make yogurt cheese.** Yogurt cheese has the same consistency as cream cheese but is much lower in fat. It can be used as a spread for bagels, toast, and crackers or as a low-calorie, low-fat, low-cholesterol substitute for cream cheese in traditional cheesecake recipes. To make yogurt cheese, empty a pint of yogurt into a large, fine-meshed strainer or colander lined with a double thickness of cheesecloth, a coffee filter, or a yogurt strainer. Place a bowl under the strainer to catch the liquid (whey) that drains from the yogurt. Cover the remaining yogurt and refrigerate for eight to 24 hours (texture will vary depending on how long it drains). Save the calcium-rich whey to use in soups and gravies. Makes about one cup yogurt cheese.

Invented

1919

The Name

Dannon is an Americanized version of Danone, the Spanish yogurt manufacturing company founded by Dr. Isaac Carasso and named for his son Daniel. Danone means "Little Daniel."

A Short History

Yogurt is believed to have originated during biblical times. A staple in the Middle East, yogurt was introduced to Europe in the sixteenth century. In Spain in 1919, Dr. Isaac Carasso perfected the first industrial manufacturing process for yogurt (using bacterial cultures developed at the Pasteur Institute in Paris) and named his company for his son Daniel. In 1942, Daniel Carasso brought the company to the United States, where he Americanized the name to Dannon.

Ingredients

Cultured grade A milk and pectin, active yogurt cultures, and *Lactobacillus acidophilus* cultures

Strange Facts

■ Yogurt is simply cultured milk. When live active cultures are added to milk, they convert the lactose into lactic acid. To label a product "yogurt," the United States Food and Drug Administration requires the use of two live active cultures,

Lactobacillus bulgaricus and *Streptococcus thermophilus*. Dannon also adds the bacteria *Lactobacillus acidophilus* to the majority of their yogurts.

■ Scientific research has shown that live active cultures boost the body's immune system and help the body digest proteins and lactose.

■ All Dannon yogurts contain at least ten million active cultures per gram.

■ Dannon plain yogurt was first sold in returnable half-pint glass jars.

■ Yogurt helps the estimated 50 million Americans who are milk intolerant—incapable of digesting lactose, the principal sugar found in milk. Because of its high levels of live active cultures, Dannon Yogurt can be eaten by lactose-intolerant people, providing them with all the nutritional benefits of milk.

■ Yogurt provides nearly one and half times more calcium than milk. A single serving of Dannon Yogurt provides 25 to 40 percent of daily calcium requirements.

■ In 1992, researchers from the University of Southern California School of Medicine in Los Angeles reported that people who ate yogurt, even as little as three to four times a month, showed lower relative risk of developing colon cancer.

Distribution

■ Dannon is the best-selling yogurt in the United States, with more than two million cups of yogurt sold every day.

■ Dannon Yogurt, with live active cultures, is available in Low Fat Fruit, Low Fat Fruit on the Bottom, Fruit on the Bottom Mini-Packs, Blended Fat Free, Blended Fat Free Mini-Packs, Tropifruta, D'Animals, Sprinkl'ins, Sprinkl'ins

Crazy Crunch, Light Fruited, Light Flavored, Light Fruited Mini-Packs, and Light 'N' Crunchy.

For More Information

The Dannon Information Center, P.O. Box 44235, Jacksonville, FL 32231-4235. Or telephone 1-800-321-2174.

Efferdent

■ **Clean a toilet bowl.** Drop several Efferdent tablets into the toilet bowl, scrub, and flush.

■ **Polish diamonds.** Drop one Efferdent tablet in a glass of water and immerse diamonds for two minutes.

■ **Clean a Thermos bottle.** Fill the bottle with water, drop in three Efferdent tablets, and let soak for an hour or longer if necessary.

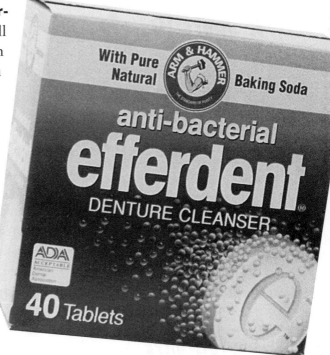

■ **Unclog a sink.** Drop several Efferdent tablets into the sink and let sit overnight.

■ **Clean a vase.** To remove a stain from the bottom of a glass vase or cruet, fill with water and drop in one Efferdent tablet.

■ **Clean hubcaps.** Drop one Efferdent tablet into a glass of water, use a cloth to apply the fizzing solution to the hubcaps, and wash clean with water.

Invented
1966

The Name
Efferdent is a combination of the words *effervesce* and *dentures*.

A Short History
The Etruscans made the earliest-known dentures, crafted from stone, wood, and animal teeth. For centuries, skilled artisans individually constructed dentures, often using gold, silver, and ivory. In 1851, following the discovery of a process to harden the juices of certain tropical plants into vulcanized rubber, porcelain teeth were embedded in gutta-percha or rubber bases. Since World War II, acrylic plastics have replaced the use of rubber and porcelain in making dentures. As with teeth, plaque buildup collects on dentures, producing bacterial odors and leading to denture stains. Throughout history, denture wearers brushed their dentures—until 1967, when Warner-Lambert introduced Efferdent, the world's first denture effervescent cleansing tablet.

Ingredients
Potassium monopersulfate compound, sodium perborate, sodium bicarbonate, citric acid, sodium carbonate, ethylene-

diamine tetraacetic acid tetrasodium salt dihydrate, lathanol, sodium tripolyphosphate, sodium benzoate, magnesium stearate, polytetrafluoroethylene powder, sodium sulfate anhydrous, mint fragrance, FD&C green no. 3, FD&C blue no. 2

Strange Facts

■ More than three billion denture cleanser tablets were sold in the United States in 1993.

■ Efferdent kills 99.9 percent of the odor-causing bacteria on dentures.

■ Paul Revere, the American patriot best remembered for his midnight ride from Boston to Lexington to herald the news of the British invasion, was also a craftsman who fashioned dentures from ivory and gold.

■ George Washington, the first president of the United States, owned at least one pair of dentures made from wood. He never used Efferdent.

Distribution

■ Five to seven million Efferdent tablets are produced daily.

■ Denture cleansers include effervescent tablets, pastes, gels, and foams. Tablets account for 81 percent of all denture cleanser sales. In 1994, Efferdent accounted for more than 38 percent of all denture cleanser tablet sales, followed by Polident with 28 percent.

For More Information

Warner-Lambert Company, 201 Tabor Road, Morris Plains, NJ 07950. Or telephone 1-800-223-0182.

Glue-All

■ **Remove a splinter.** Coat the splinter with a drop of Elmer's Glue-All, wait for it to dry, then peel off the dried glue. The splinter should be stuck to it.

■ **Seal plants.** Gardeners use Elmer's Glue-All to seal ends of pruned stems and branches against insects and excessive moisture loss.

■ **Prevent broken shoelaces from fraying.** Dip the ends into Elmer's Glue-All.

■ **Fix small holes in walls.** Small nail holes can be filled by squirting in a drop of Elmer's Glue-All before painting.

■ **Make moldable dough that dries without baking.** Mix equal parts Elmer's Glue-All, flour, and cornstarch. Mix and knead well until blended. If too dry, add more glue. If too moist, add more flour and cornstarch. Food coloring may be added if desired. Dough can be molded into any desired shape to create animals, figurines, ornaments, and jewelry. Dough keeps for weeks in a Ziploc Storage Bag.

■ **Tighten a screw hole.** When a screw hole is too worn out to hold a screw, soak a cotton ball in Elmer's Glue-All, stuff it into the hole, and let dry for 24 hours. Use a screwdriver to put a new screw into the spot.

■ **Make a starch fabric stiffener.** Mix water and Elmer's Glue-All in a bowl to desired consistency. Fabric dipped in the mixture can be shaped and dried in decorative forms and shapes.

■ **Teach kids how to write their name.** Use crayon to write the child's name on a piece of paper, then trace over the letters using Elmer's Glue-All. When the glue dries, children can use their fingers to trace along the tactile letters of their names, making it easier to understand the shapes of the letters.

Invented
1947

The Name
In 1936, Borden launched a series of advertisements featuring cartoon cows, including Elsie, the spokescow for Borden dairy products. In 1940, compelled by Elsie's popularity, Borden dressed up "You'll Do Lobelia," a seven-year-old 950-pound Jersey cow from Brookfield, MA, as Elsie for an exhibit at the World's Fair. She stood in a barn boudoir decorated with

whimsical props, including churns used as tables, lamps made from milk bottles, a wheelbarrow for a chaise longue, and oil paintings of Elsie's ancestors—among them Great-Aunt Bess in her bridal gown and Uncle Bosworth, the noted Spanish-American War admiral. This attracted the attention of RKO Pictures, which hired Elsie to star with Jack Oakie and Kay Francis in the movie *Little Men*. Borden needed to find a replacement for Elsie at the World's Fair exhibit. Elsie's husband, Elmer, was chosen, and the boudoir was converted overnight into a bachelor apartment, complete with every conceivable prop to suggest a series of nightly poker parties. In 1951, Borden chose Elmer to be the marketing symbol for all of Borden's glues and adhesives.

A Short History

In 1929, the Borden Co. purchased the Casein Co. of America, the leading manufacturer of glues made from casein, a milk by-product. Borden introduced its first nonfood consumer product, Casco Glue, in 1932. After World War II, Borden expanded into synthetic resin glues that did not use casein. The product known today as Elmer's Glue-All was first introduced in 1947 under the brand name Cascorez, packaged in two-ounce glass jars with wooden applicators. Sales did not take off until 1951, when Elsie's husband, Elmer, was chosen as the marketing symbol. In 1952, Borden repackaged Glue-All into the familiar plastic squeeze bottle with the orange applicator top.

Ingredients

Polyvinyl acetate dispersed in water

Strange Facts

■ The Elmer's line now includes nearly 150 types and sizes of adhesives, caulks, and specialty items.

■ Elsie the Cow and her husband, Elmer, have two calves, Beulah and Beauregard.

Distribution

■ Elmer's Glue-All is the best-selling glue in America.

■ Borden's Elmer's Glue operation in Bainbridge, NY, produces approximately 35 million four-ounce bottles of Elmer's Glue-All, School Glue, and GluColors annually.

For More Information

Borden, Inc., Columbus, OH 43215. Or telephone 1-800-426-7336.

■ **Revive an ailing houseplant.** Give the plant two tablespoons Geritol twice a week for three months. New leaves
should begin to grow within the first month.

■ **Polish shoes.** In a pinch, you can shine your brown
leather shoes with a few drops of Geritol on a soft cloth.

■ **Remove stains, rings, and minor scratches from
wood furniture.** Apply Geritol to the wood with a cotton
ball, wipe away excess, and polish as usual.

Invented
1950

The Name
Geritol is apparently a combination of the words *geriatric* and
tolerance.

A Short History
Geritol liquid tonic was introduced in 1950 by Pharmaceuticals Inc. as a remedy for those who felt tired because of iron-
poor blood. With Ralph Bellamy and Ted Mack touting
Geritol's unique ability to prevent iron-poor blood, Geritol

quickly became the number one high-potency iron tonic in America. Pharmaceuticals Inc. sold Geritol to the J. B. Williams Company, which reformulated Geritol in 1967 to include high-potency iron plus seven vitamins, targeting women with iron-poor blood.

Geritol remained the best-selling iron and vitamin supplement until 1979, when health-conscious consumers began seeking more complete vitamin formulas. In 1982, Beecham acquired J. B. Williams and the following year introduced New, Improved Geritol with high-potency iron plus nine vitamins and minerals. Beecham reformulated Geritol again in 1984 as Geritol Complete with iron plus 29 vitamins and minerals, repositioning Geritol as a multivitamin and multimineral supplement—adding beta carotene in 1988.

The following year Beecham merged with SmithKline Beckman to form SmithKline Beecham, and in 1993, the company completely repositioned Geritol as a high-potency multivitamin/multimineral supplement, reducing the amount of iron in Geritol to one-third the original formula.

Ingredients

ACTIVE: iron (ferric ammonium citrate), thiamine, riboflavin, niacinamide, panthenol, pyridoxine, cyanocobalamin, methionine, choline bitartrate; INACTIVE: twelve percent alcohol, benzoic acid, caramel color, citric acid, invert sugar, sucrose, water, flavors

Strange Facts

■ While one dose of the original formula for Geritol contained twice the iron in a pound of calf's liver, today one dose of Geritol Complete contains approximately two-thirds the iron in a pound of calf's liver.

■ In 1956, Geritol sponsored *Twenty-One*, the game show featured in the 1994 Hollywood Pictures movie *Quiz Show*, directed by Robert Redford and recounting the game show scandal in which producers fed answers to contestants.

■ In 1971, Geritol launched the television commercial that created the catchphrase "My Wife, I Think I'll Keep Her," which, in 1994, provided the inspiration for the Mary-Chapin Carpenter song "He Thinks He'll Keep Her."

■ Wimbledon tennis champion Evonne Goolagong supplemented her on-court activities with Geritol tablets.

■ In 1989, after challenging heavyweight champion Mike Tyson to a fight for the title, former heavyweight champion George Foreman told *Time* magazine, "If I win, every man over forty can grab his Geritol and have a toast."

■ Geritol, at less than one calorie per tablet, contains no sodium, sugar, lactose, artificial sweeteners, or preservatives.

■ Three out of four people surveyed in 1994 said Bob Barker is the TV game show host most likely to take Geritol.

Distribution

■ SmithKline Beecham sells more than 300 products in 130 countries.

■ Geritol accounts for less than two percent of SmithKline Beecham's sales.

■ SmithKline Beecham sells two of the world's top ten medicines (the anti-ulcer drug Tagamet and the antibiotic Augmentin) and a slew of well-known consumer products including Contac, Tums, Sucrets, Aqua-Fresh, and Brylcreem.

For More Information

Beecham Products, Division of Beecham, Inc., Pittsburgh, PA 15230. Or telephone 1-800-245-1040. In PA, telephone 1-800-242-1718.

Heinz Vinegar

■ **Milk cows organically.** Clean milking equipment with unperfumed dish detergent followed with a Heinz Vinegar rinse. Pipes, hoses, and bulk tank will come out squeaky clean without any odor, lowering the bacteria count.

■ **Kill bacteria in meats.** Marinating meat in Heinz Vinegar kills bacteria and tenderizes the meat. Use one-quarter cup vinegar for a two- to three-pound roast, marinate overnight, then cook without draining or rinsing the meat. Add herbs to the vinegar when marinating as desired.

■ **Dissolve warts.** Mix one part Heinz Apple Cider Vinegar to one part glycerin into a lotion and apply daily to warts until they dissolve.

■ **Remove stubborn stains from furniture upholstery and clothes.** Apply Heinz White Vinegar directly to the stain, then wash as directed by the manufacturer's instructions.

■ **Grow beautiful azaleas.** Occasionally water plants with a mixture of two tablespoons Heinz Vinegar to one quart water. Azaleas grow best in acidic soil.

■ **Relieve arthritis.** Before each meal, drink a glass of water containing two teaspoons Heinz Apple Cider Vinegar. Give this folk remedy at least three weeks to start working.

■ **Kill unwanted grass.** Pour Heinz White Vinegar in crevices and between bricks.

■ **Remove corns.** Make a poultice of one crumbled piece of bread soaked in one-quarter cup Heinz Vinegar. Let poultice sit for one-half hour, then apply to corn and tape in place overnight. If corn does not peel off by morning, reapply the poultice for several consecutive nights.

■ **Clean the hoses and unclog soap scum from a washing machine.** Once a month pour one cup Heinz White Vinegar into the washing machine and run through a normal cycle, without clothes.

■ **Cure an upset stomach.** Drink two teaspoons Heinz Apple Cider Vinegar in one cup water to soothe an upset stomach.

■ **Kill germs on bathroom fixtures.** Use one part Heinz Vinegar to one part water in a spray bottle. Spray the bathroom fixtures and floor, then wipe clean.

■ **Clean soap scum, mildew, and grime from bathtub, tile, and shower curtains.** Simply wipe the surface with Heinz Vinegar and rinse with water.

■ **Deodorize the air.** Heinz Vinegar is a natural air freshener when sprayed in a room.

■ **Relieve itching.** Use a cotton ball to dab mosquito and other bug bites with Heinz Vinegar straight from the bottle.

■ **Clean lime deposits and calcium sludge from an automatic drip coffeemaker.** Once a month fill the reservoir with Heinz White Vinegar and run through the brew cycle. Rinse thoroughly with two cycles of cold water.

■ **Relieve a sore throat.** Put two teaspoons Heinz Vinegar in your humidifier.

■ **Soothe sunburn pain.** Apply undiluted Heinz Vinegar to the burn.

■ **Clean food-stained pots and pans.** Fill the pots and pans with Heinz White Vinegar and let stand for 30 minutes, then rinse in hot, soapy water.

■ **Clean rust from tools, bolts, and spigots.** Soak the rusted tool, bolt, or spigot in undiluted Heinz White Vinegar overnight.

■ **Turn a chicken bone into rubber.** Soak a chicken bone in a glass of Heinz Vinegar for three days. It will bend like rubber.

■ **Prevent bright-colored clothes from fading.** Before putting the article in the washing machine, soak it in Heinz White Vinegar for ten minutes.

■ **Keep a garbage disposal clean and smelling fresh.**
Mix one cup Heinz Vinegar in enough water to fill an ice-cube tray, freeze the mixture, grind the cubes through the disposal, and flush with cold water.

■ **Clean a toilet bowl.** Pour in one cup Heinz White Vinegar, let stand for five minutes, and flush.

■ **Prevent yeast infections.** Douche with one tablespoon Heinz White Vinegar to one quart warm water to adjust the pH balance in the vagina.

■ **Clean dentures.** Soak dentures overnight in Heinz White Vinegar, then brush off tartar with a toothbrush.

■ **Remove perspiration stains from clothes.** Apply one part Heinz White Vinegar to four parts water, then rinse.

■ **Deodorize a room filled with cigarette smoke or paint fumes.** Place a small bowl of Heinz White Vinegar in the room.

■ **Cure the hiccups.** Mix one teaspoon Heinz Apple Cider Vinegar in one cup warm water and drink.

■ **Eliminate odors from used jars.** Rinse peanut butter and mayonnaise jars with Heinz White Vinegar.

■ **Condition dry hair.** Shampoo, then rinse hair with a mixture of one cup Heinz Apple Cider Vinegar and two cups water. Vinegar adds highlights to brunette hair, restores the acid mantel, and removes soap film and sebum oil.

■ **Clean mineral deposits from a steam iron.** Fill the water tank with Heinz White Vinegar. Turn the iron to the steam setting and steam-iron a soft utility rag to clean the steam ports. Repeat the process with water, then thoroughly rinse out the inside of your iron.

■ **Remove light scorch marks from fabrics.** Rub lightly with Heinz White Vinegar, then wipe with a clean cloth.

■ **Repel ants.** Use a spray bottle or mister filled with a solution of equal parts Heinz Vinegar and water around doorjambs, window-sills, water pipes, and foundation cracks.

■ **Keep drains open.** Pour one-half box old baking soda down the drain, followed by one cup Heinz White Vinegar. When the bub-bling stops, run the hot water.

■ **Prolong and brighten pro-pane lanterns.** Soak new wicks for several hours in Heinz White Vinegar and let dry before insert-ing. Propane lanterns will burn longer and brighter on the same amount of fuel.

■ **Remove decals or bumper stickers.** Soak a cloth in Heinz Vin-egar and cover the decal or bumper sticker for several minutes until the vinegar soaks in. The decals and bumper stickers should peel off easily.

■ **Deodorize a wool sweater.** Wash sweater, then rinse in equal parts Heinz Vinegar and water.

■ **Prevent lint from clinging to clothes.** Add one cup Heinz Vinegar to the wash load.

■ **Prevent ice from forming on a car windshield overnight.** Coat the window with a solution of three parts Heinz White or Apple Cider Vinegar to one part water.

■ **Prolong the life of flowers in a vase.** Add two tablespoons Heinz White Vinegar plus three tablespoons sugar per quart of warm water. Stems should be in three to four inches of water.

■ **Prevent cracked hard-boiled eggs.** Add two tablespoons Heinz White Vinegar per quart of water before boiling to prevent the eggs from cracking. The eggshells will also peel off faster and easier.

■ **Clean windows.** Use undiluted Heinz Vinegar in a spray bottle. Dry with a soft cloth.

■ **Eliminate cooking odors in the kitchen.** Boil one tablespoon Heinz White Vinegar with one cup water.

■ **Remove wallpaper.** Mix equal parts Heinz Vinegar and hot water. Use a paint roller to wet the paper thoroughly with the mixture. Repeat. Paper should peel off in sheets.

■ **Eliminate animal urine stains from carpet.** Blot up urine, flush several times with lukewarm water, then apply a mixture of equal parts Heinz White Vinegar and cool water. Blot up, rinse, and let dry.

■ **Relieve a cold.** Mix one-quarter cup Heinz Apple Cider Vinegar with one-quarter cup honey. Take one tablespoon six to eight times daily.

■ **Deodorize a stale lunch box.** Soak a paper napkin in Heinz Vinegar and leave it inside the closed lunch box overnight.

■ **Prevent soapy film on glassware.** Place a cup of Heinz White Vinegar on the bottom rack of your dishwasher, run for five minutes, then run though the full cycle. A cup of white vinegar run through the entire cycle once a month will also reduce soap scum on the inner workings.

■ **Unclog a showerhead.** Unscrew the showerhead, re-move the rubber washer, place the head in a pot filled with equal parts Heinz Vinegar and water, bring to a boil, then simmer for five minutes.

■ **Relieve a cough.** Mix one-half cup Heinz Apple Cider Vinegar, one-half cup water, one teaspoon cayenne pepper, and four teaspoons honey. Take one tablespoon when cough acts up. Take another tablespoon at bedtime.

■ **Retard patching plaster from drying.** Add one table-spoon Heinz White Vinegar to the water when mixing plaster to slow the drying time.

Invented
1880

The Name
Vinegar is derived from two French words, *vin* (wine) and *aigre* (sour).

A Short History
Since wine originated at least 10,000 years ago, the first vinegar most likely resulted from spoiled wine. In 5000 B.C., the Babylonians fermented vinegar from date palms, enhancing the flavor by adding tarragon, ruta, absinth, lavender, mint, celery, portulaca, and saffron. Heinz Vinegars were first bottled in 1880, using no additives or preservatives. Vinegar's key ingredient is alcohol. Unlike many budget-brand vinegars that derive their alcohol content from petroleum, Heinz vinegars use only sun-ripened corn or apples and water.

Ingredients
DISTILLED WHITE VINEGAR: select sun-ripened grain, diluted with water to a uniform pickling and table strength of five percent (50 grains) acidity; APPLE CIDER VINEGAR: the juice of apples, diluted with water to a uniform pickling and table strength of five percent (50 grains) acidity

Strange Facts

■ Vinegar can be made from virtually any sugary substance that can be fermented to ethyl alcohol, including molasses, sorghum syrup, fruits, berries, melons, coconut, honey, maple syrup, potatoes, beets, malt, grains, and whey. The oldest way to make vinegar is to leave wine made from fruit juice in an open container, allowing microorganisms in the air to convert the ethyl alcohol to acetic acid.

■ In 1992, H. J. Heinz hired its first spokesperson for vinegar, Heloise Cruise Evan, the syndicated columnist who writes "Hints from Heloise." "I probably use a gallon a week," Heloise told the *Wall Street Journal*.

■ Vinegar lasts indefinitely in the pantry without refrigeration.

■ White vinegar is used to pickle vegetables and fruits. Vinegar neutralizes all the water in vegetables and fruits while leaving enough behind to preserve them. Heinz publishes a 32-page booklet with recipes for canning and pickling vegetables and fruits. For a free copy, write to *Heinz Successful Pickling Guide*, P.O. Box 57, Pittsburgh, PA 15230.

■ Hannibal, the Carthaginian general, used vinegar to help clear boulders blocking the path of his elephants across the alps. Titus Livius reported in *The History of Rome* that Hannibal's soldiers heated the rocks and applied vinegar to split them.

■ According to the *New Testament*, Roman soldiers offered a sponge filled with vinegar to Jesus on the cross. While the act is usually considered cruel, vinegar actually shuts off the taste buds, temporarily quenching thirst, suggesting that the Roman soldiers may have been acting out of kindness.

■ Vinegar has served medicinal purposes since biblical times, when it was used as a wet dressing on wounds. Hippocrates, the father of medicine, used vinegar on his patients in 400 B.C. The Assyrians used vinegar to topically treat middle-ear infections, and during World War I vinegar was used to treat wounds.

Distribution
■ The *Progressive Grocer* reported that supermarket sales of vinegar average $112 million a year.

For More Information
■ H. J. Heinz Co., P.O. Box 57, Pittsburgh, PA 15230. Or telephone 1-412-456-5700.

■ Vinegar Institute, Suite 500G, 5775 Peachtree-Dunwoody Road, Atlanta, GA 30342. Or telephone 1-404-252-3663.

Soap

■ **Repulse deer.** Hang bars of Ivory soap around crops.

■ **Lubricate a handsaw blade.** Rub Ivory soap across the sides and teeth of the saw to help the blade glide through wood.

■ **Make bubble bath.** Hold a bar of Ivory soap under running water to fill the tub with bubbles.

■ **Fix small holes in walls.** Rub a bar of Ivory soap over the hole until it looks filled, then paint.

■ **Lubricate zippers.** Rub the teeth of the zipper with a bar of Ivory soap to make the zipper glide easier.

■ **Prevent campfire soot from sticking to the bottom of pots and pans.** Lightly rub the bottoms of pots and pans with a bar of Ivory soap before using them over an open fire.

■ **Lubricate nails and screws.** Nails and screws rubbed with Ivory soap will go into wood easier.

■ **Stop insect bites from itching.** Dab the bite with a wet bar of Ivory soap and let dry to desensitize the skin.

■ **Make a pincushion.** Using a wrapped bar of Ivory soap as a pincushion makes needles glide through fabric.

■ **Keep clothes and linens smelling fresh.** Place an unwrapped bar of Ivory soap in drawers, linen closets, and storage trunks.

■ **Lubricate furniture drawers and windows.** Rub Ivory soap on the casters of drawers and windows so they slide open and shut easily.

Invented
1878

The Name

Harley Procter, considering a long list of new names for his white soap, was inspired one Sunday morning in church when the pastor read Psalm 45: "All thy garments smell of myrrh, and aloes, and cassia, out of the ivory palaces, whereby they have made thee glad." A few years later, a chemist's analysis of Ivory soap indicated that 56/1000 of the ingredients did not fall into the category of pure soap. Procter subtracted from 1000, and wrote the slogan "99-44/100% Pure," which first appeared in Ivory's advertising in 1882. "It Floats" was added to Ivory's slogan in 1891.

A Short History

When Harley Procter decided to develop a creamy white soap to compete with imported castile soaps, he asked his cousin, chemist James Gamble, to formulate the product. One day after the soap went into production, a factory worker (who remains anonymous) forgot to switch off the master mixing machine when he went to lunch, and too much air was whipped into a batch of soap. Consumers, delighted by the floating soap, demanded more, and from then on, Procter and Gamble gave all white soap an extra-long whipping.

Ingredients

Vegetable oils, animals fats, fragrance, and less than 0.5 percent magnesium sulfate and sodium silicate

Strange Facts

■ Ivory soap is the best-selling soap in America because the air-laden bars dissolve twice as fast as other brands, compelling consumers to buy twice as much.

Distribution

■ Approximately 30 billion cakes of Ivory soap had been manufactured by 1990.

For More Information

Procter & Gamble Co., 391 East 6th Street, Cincinnati, OH 45202. Or telephone 1-800-262-1637.

Peanut Butter

■ **Shave.** Former senator Barry Goldwater of Arizona once shaved with peanut butter while on a camping trip. (For best results, avoid shaving with Jif Extra Crunchy.)

■ **Remove bubblegum from hair.** Rub a dollop of Jif peanut butter into the bubblegum.

■ **Remove airplane glue or cement glue from furniture.** Simply rub the dried glue with Jif peanut butter.

■ **Grease a car or truck axle.** George Washington Carver developed axle grease from peanuts.

■ **Make peanut soup.** Peanut butter is the main ingredient in any recipe for peanut soup.

■ **Trap mice or rats.** Bait a trap with Jif peanut butter.

Invented

1956

The Name

Jif is short for *jiffy*, the amount of time it takes to make a peanut butter sandwich.

A Short History

For centuries, African tribes and the Incas ate a paste made from peanuts. In 1890, Dr. Ambrose W. Straub of St. Louis, MO, crushed peanuts into a paste for his geriatric patients with bad teeth. In 1903, Straub received the patent for a machine that ground peanuts into butter, unveiling his invention at the 1904 World's Fair in St. Louis. By 1914, there were several dozen brands on the market. Procter & Gamble introduced Jif in 1956, and today Jif is the top-selling peanut butter in America.

Ingredients

Roasted peanuts, sugar, and two percent or less of: molasses, partially hydrogenated vegetable oil (soybean), fully hydrogenated vegetable oils (rapeseed and soybean), mono- and diglycerides, and salt

Strange Facts

■ Jif does not require refrigeration and will stay fresh for approximately three months after opening.

- A 28-ounce jar of Jif contains 1,218 peanuts.
- The Jif plant in Lexington, KY, is reportedly the largest peanut butter factory in the world.
- The peanut is a member of the pea family.
- Peanut butter sticks to the roof of your mouth because its high protein content draws moisture from your mouth.
- Peanut butter is the most commonly used form of the peanut. Half of America's 1.6-million-ton annual peanut crop is used to make peanut butter.
- As president of the United States, Gerald Ford had peanut butter on an English muffin for breakfast every morning.
- Jimmy Carter was the first peanut farmer elected president of the United States.
- According to *Americana* magazine, the average high school graduate has eaten 1,500 peanut butter and jelly sandwiches.
- The average jar of peanut butter is consumed in less than thirty days.
- Pound for pound, peanuts have more protein, minerals, and vitamins than beef liver.
- The Adults Only Peanut-Butter Lovers Fan Club publishes a newsletter called *Spread the News*, hosts annual conventions for peanut butter fanatics, and distributes peanut butter recipes.

Unusual Events

- Every October, Suffolk, VA, stages a peanut festival featuring the World's Only Peanut Butter Sculpture Contest, offering a prize for the best sculpture made entirely of peanut butter.

Distribution

- Americans eat 170 million pounds of Jif every year. That's enough to make two billion peanut butter sandwiches.

■ Nearly 120 billion peanuts are used to make the amount of Jif peanut butter produced in one year.

■ According to the Peanut Advisory Board, 83 percent of all Americans purchase peanut butter.

■ One out of every ten peanuts grown in the United States for domestic consumption ends up in a jar of Jif.

■ Procter & Gamble makes Jif Creamy, Jif Extra Crunchy, Simply Jif Creamy (low sugar and low salt), Simply Jif Extra Crunchy, and Jif Reduced Fat Creamy.

For More Information

■ Procter & Gamble Co., P.O. Box 5561, Cincinnati, OH 45201. Or telephone 1-800-283-8915.

■ National Peanut Council, 1500 King Street, Suite 301, Alexandria, VA 22314. Or telephone 1-703-838-9500.

Charcoal Briquets

■ **Prevent tools from rusting.** Placing a charcoal briquet in a toolbox helps absorb moisture, according to household-hints columnist Mary Ellen.

■ **Freshen air in a closed space.** Placing a coffee can filled with charcoal briquets in a closet or chest helps absorb odors, according to *Reader's Digest*.

■ **Deodorize your refrigerator.** A cup of charcoal briquets in the back of the refrigerator helps keep it smelling fresh and clean, according to Mary Ellen.

Invented
Early 1920s

The Name
Ford Charcoal was renamed Kingsford Charcoal Briquets after E.G. Kingsford, the relative who helped Henry Ford select the site for his charcoal plant.

A Short History
In the early 1920s, Henry Ford wanted to find a use for the growing piles of wood scraps from the production of his

Model Ts. Ford learned of a process for turning the wood scraps into charcoal briquets, and one of his relatives, E.G. Kingsford, helped select the site for Ford's charcoal plant. Essentially, wood scraps are heated in ovens that contain little or no air, causing the hydrogen, nitrogen, and oxygen in the wood to escape, leaving behind black, porous wood char. The company town which sprang up around the site was named in Kingsford's honor, and in 1951, Ford Charcoal was renamed Kingsford Charcoal.

Ingredients

Wood char (contributes barbecue flavor), mineral char (to make the briquets burn longer), limestone (to give the briquets a white ash appearance when they're ready), sodium nitrate (to help the briquets ignite quickly), starch (binder)

Strange Facts

■ Kingsford turns approximately one million tons of wood waste into a usable product—charcoal briquets—every year.

■ *Fortune* magazine rated Kingsford Charcoal Briquets one of the best products made in America.

■ Charcoal briquets for barbecuing should not be confused with activated charcoal, manufactured by other companies that remove most of the impurities from ordinary charcoal by treating it with steam and air heated to above 600°F. While wood, bone, and activated charcoal are all used to absorb colors, flavors, and odors from gases and liquids, activated charcoal—available in pet stores (for fish tank filters) and drug stores (in capsule form)—works best.

■ Activated charcoal allegedly helps dry up acne pimples,

according to Ben Harris, author of *Kitchen Medicines*, who suggests taking one-half teaspoon of activated charcoal three times a day after meals.

■ In May 1959, the United States sent two young female monkeys, Able and Baker, into space in a *Jupiter* rocket. Monkey Able, dressed in a space suit, wore gauze and charcoal diapers.

■ On July 20, 1969, Neil Armstrong, the first man on the moon, spoke the first words on the moon: "That's one small step for man, one giant leap for mankind." The second thought he expressed was: "The surface is fine and powdery, it adheres in fine layers, like powdered charcoal, to the soles and sides of my foot."

■ All automobile engines contain a canister filled with activated charcoal that absorbs evaporating gasoline fumes when the car's engine is off. The system is designed to prevent hydrocarbons from being released into the atmosphere by trapping and storing fuel vapor from the fuel tank, the carburetor, or the fuel injection system.

Distribution

■ The Kingsford Product Company remains the leading manufacturer of charcoal in the United States, converting more than one million tons of wood scraps into charcoal briquets each year.

■ More than 77 percent of all households in the United States own a barbecue grill. Nearly half of those grill owners barbecue year round and, on the average, use their grills five times a month.

For More Information

The Kingsford Products Co., Oakland, CA 94623.

Sheer Energy

■ **Find a contact lens on the floor or carpet.** Cover your vacuum-hose nozzle carefully with a piece of L'eggs hose and a rubber band to keep the lens from being sucked in. Gently vacuum with the nozzle one inch above the floor.

■ **Strain lumps from paint.** Stretch a L'eggs Sheer Energy panty hose across the paint can and pour.

■ **Shine a wood floor.** Insert a folded bath towel into one leg of the stocking and hand buff the floor.

■ **Apply wood stain, varnish, or polyurethane.** Old L'eggs make great substitutes for paintbrushes. Ball up the panty hose and use it like a sponge or secure it to a stick with several rubber bands.

■ **Clean dentures.** Cut a small piece of nylon from the L'eggs and polish dentures.

■ **Scrub your back with soap.** Place a bar of soap inside one leg of a pair of L'eggs Sheer Energy at the knee, tie knots on both sides of it, hold one end of the stocking in each hand, and seesaw it across your back in the bathtub.

■ **Prevent lint from sticking to clothes in the dryer.** Throw a pair of L'eggs into the dryer with your wet clothes.

■ **Secure garbage bags inside your trash can.** Cut off the elastic top of a pair of L'eggs Sheer Energy and stretch the extra-large rubber band around the rim of the trash can to hold the plastic garbage bag in place.

■ **Remove excess plaster after filling a hole.** Scrub with a balled-up pair of L'eggs.

■ **Make a catnip ball.** Stuff the toe of a L'eggs stocking with catnip and knot it.

■ **Clean dust from window screens.** Simply run a balled-up pair of L'eggs over the screen.

■ **Wash bottles.** Wrap a section of a L'eggs around the bristles of a bottle brush, fasten with a rubber band, and scrub.

■ **Secure mothballs.** Use a L'eggs stocking to hold mothballs in the closet.

■ **Store plant bulbs, onions, or garlic.** Fill the foot of a pair of L'eggs Sheer Energy and hang it high to keep the contents dry.

- **Clean the sink, bathtub, and bathroom tiles.** Use a balled-up pair of L'eggs as a non-abrasive scouring pad.

- **Tie tomato plants to stakes.** The soft nylon of L'eggs Sheer Energy secures tomato stalks without causing any damage to the plant.

- **Clean your windows.** Use a balled-up pair of L'eggs.

- **Clean the dust from under the refrigerator.** Place one stocking leg over the end of a broomstick and secure with a rubber band. Slide the broomstick under the refrigerator and move it back and forth.

- **Prevent soil from leaking out of a potted plant.** Place a pair of L'eggs Sheer Energy in the bottom of plant pots to provide drainage.

- **Remove dead insects from the hood of the car.** Use a damp, balled-up pair of L'eggs to clean the car without scratching the finish.

Invented
1970

The Name
A clever combination of the words *legs* and *eggs*, with an apostrophe added to make the wordplay idiot-proof.

A Short History

At the 1939 World's Fair, Dupont introduced nylon stockings to the world. On May 15, 1940, they were available in stores. Nineteen years later, Glen Raven Mills of North Carolina introduced panty hose, eventually developing a seamless model just in time for the advent of the miniskirt in 1965. In 1970, Hanes creatively packaged panty hose in plastic eggs in supermarkets, drugstores, and convenience stores—places where they had never been available before. Sheer Energy was introduced in 1973 as the first L'eggs panty hose made with sheer spandex yarn. In 1991, L'eggs replaced the plastic egg with a cardboard package to reduce waste. While the plastic eggs were recyclable and used for arts-and-crafts projects, the new box, using 38 percent less material and made from recycled paper, allows 33 percent more containers to fit into the store display rack and is still rounded at the top like an egg.

Ingredients

PANTY: 90 percent nylon, 10 percent spandex; LEG: 80 percent nylon, 20 percent spandex; GUSSET: 55 percent cotton, 45 percent polyester

Strange Facts

■ In the 1970s, when Peter Lynch, the most successful money manager in America, noticed his wife, Carolyn, bringing L'eggs panty hose home from the supermarket, his Fidelity Magellan fund bought stock in Hanes. The value of its shares rose nearly 600 percent.

- L'eggs supported the women of the 1994 and 1996 United States Olympic Teams.

Distribution

- L'eggs is the best-selling panty hose in America.
- 97 percent of all supermarkets, drugstores, and convenience stores in the United States carry L'eggs panty hose.
- The full line of L'eggs products includes L'eggs Regular, L'eggs Control Top, L'eggs Classics, L'eggs Sheer Energy, L'eggs Sheer Elegance, L'eggs Silken Mist, L'eggs Active Support, L'eggs Everyday, L'eggs Just My Size, and L'eggs Silky Support Smooth Silhouettes.

For More Information

L'eggs Products, P.O. Box 2495, Winston-Salem, NC 27102. Or telephone 1-800-92-LEGGS.

Listerine

■ **Cure acne.** Use a cotton ball to dab Listerine on blemishes.

■ **Fertilize a lawn.** Jerry Baker, author of *The Impatient Gardener,* suggests one cup Epsom and one cup am- mixing one cup Listerine, salts, one cup liquid soap, monia in a one-quart jar, filling the rest of the jar with beer. Spray this on up to 2,500 square feet of lawn with a hose-at-tached sprayer in May and again in late June.

■ **Use as a deodorant.** Listerine helps kill the bacteria that cause perspiration odor. Dab it under your arms.

■ **Eliminate mildew odors.** Wipe with full-strength Listerine.

■ **Disinfect wounds.** Listerine works as an astringent when poured on a laceration or abrasion.

■ **Disinfect a washing machine at a Laundromat.** To avoid getting germs from another family, wipe off the surface of the machine with Listerine and add one-half cup Listerine to the wash cycle.

■ **Prevent dandruff.** Wash your hair with Listerine.

Invented
1879

The Name
Listerine was named in honor of Sir Joseph Lister, the nineteenth-century British surgeon who pioneered sanitary operating room procedures.

A Short History
Impressed by Sir Joseph Lister's views on germs and his plea for "antiseptic surgery," Dr. Joseph Lawrence developed Listerine in his St. Louis laboratory as a safe and effective antiseptic for use in surgical procedures. The local Lambert Pharmacal Company manufactured Listerine exclusively for the medical profession and, in 1895, extended the sale and promotion of Listerine to the dental profession as an anti-bacterial mouthwash and gargle. In 1914, compelled by popular demand, Lambert made Listerine available to the general public.

Ingredients

ACTIVE: thymol 0.064 percent, eucalyptol 0.092 percent, methyl salicylate 0.06 percent, menthol 0.042 percent; INACTIVE: water, alcohol 26.9 percent, bentoic acid, poloxamer 40 percent, and caramel

Strange Facts

■ Listerine is the only over-the-counter brand of mouthwash clinically proven to help prevent and reduce supragingival plaque accumulation and gingivitis when used in a conscientiously applied program of oral hygiene and regular professional care.
■ Listerine should not be swallowed or administered to children under twelve years of age because it contains 26.9 percent pharmaceutical-grade alcohol.

Distribution

■ Listerine is the best-selling brand of mouthwash in the United States.
■ Listerine can be found in one out of every five homes in the United States.
■ Listerine is available in regular, Cool Mint, and FreshBurst.

For More Information

Warner-Lambert Co., 201 Tabor Road, Morris Plains, NJ 07950. Or telephone 1-800-LISTERINE.

Maybelline

Crystal Clear Nail Polish

■ **Stop a run in nylons.** Paint the snag immediately with Maybelline Crystal Clear Nail Polish.

■ **Prevent the bottom edges of shaving cream cans from rusting.** Paint the bottom rim of the can with Maybelline Crystal Clear Nail Polish.

■ **Thread a needle with ease.** Dip the end of the thread in Maybelline Crystal Clear Nail Polish, let dry, and thread.

■ **Protect shirt buttons.** Dab the center of each button with Maybelline Crystal Clear Nail Polish to reinforce the threads so buttons stay on longer.

■ **Prevent cut fabric from fraying.** Apply a thin coat of Maybelline Crystal Clear Nail Polish along seam edges to help prevent unraveling.

■ **Laminate prescription labels.** Keep prescription labels legible by painting them with Maybelline Crystal Clear Nail Polish.

■ **Repair a small dent in a window, car windshield, or wood floor.** Fill hole with a few drops of Maybelline Crystal Clear Nail Polish, let dry, then repeat until full.

■ **Prevent the knots of small ribbons on lingerie from untying.** Dab the knots with Maybelline Crystal Clear Nail Polish.

■ **Tighten loose dresser-drawer knobs.** Dip the end of the screw in Maybelline Crystal Clear Nail Polish, replace the knob, and let dry for a snug fit.

■ **Prevent rust on toilet seat screws.** Paint the screws with Maybelline Crystal Clear Nail Polish.

■ **Keep belt buckles shiny.** Paint Maybelline Crystal Clear Nail Polish on the buckle, let dry, and repeat four times.

Invented

1970s

The Name

T. L. Williams named his company in honor of his oldest sister, Mabel, who inspired him to produce an easy-to-use mascara, combining her name with the popular suffix -*line*.

The letter *y* was apparently added to make the spelling and pronunciation of the company name phonetic.

A Short History

In 3000 B.C., Chinese artists combined gum arabic, egg white, gelatin, and beeswax to create varnishes, enamels, and lacquers—which Chinese aristocrats started applying to their fingernails as a status symbol. The Maybelline Company, founded in 1915 by T. L. Williams, introduced Maybelline Cake Mascara in 1917, advertising in magazines and selling the mascara only by mail. In September 1932, Maybelline finally made mascara available in variety stores, followed by eye shadows and eye pencils. In the early 1960s, Maybelline introduced Ultra Lash, the first mass-market automatic mascara. In 1967, Williams sold his company to Plough, Inc., which became Schering-Plough Corp. in 1971. Maybelline introduced Great Lash mascara in 1973 and soon branched into other face, lip, and nail products—including a line of nail polishes. In 1992, Maybelline became a publicly held company.

Ingredients

Butyl acetate, ethyl acetate, nitrocellulose, polyester resin, sucrose acetate isobutyrate, isopropyl alcohol, camphor, acrylates copolymer, benzophenone-1, violet no. 2

Strange Facts

■ The cosmetics industry in the United States includes face makeup (representing 35 percent of sales in 1992), eye cosmetics (30 percent), lip products (23 percent), and nail products (12 percent).

■ Maybelline's Great Lash mascara has been the best-selling mascara in the United States since its introduction in 1973.

Distribution

■ Maybelline markets cosmetics in the United States and 40 international markets (including Indonesia, Peru, Nicaragua, and Iceland) plus the Yardley line of soaps and bath-care products in the United States and Canada.

■ In 1993, Maybelline's consolidated net sales were more than $346 million.

■ In the United States, Maybelline is the number two cosmetics company, behind Cover Girl and ahead of Revlon.

For More Information

Maybelline, Inc., 3030 Jackson Avenue, Memphis, TN 38112-2018. Or telephone 1-901-324-0310.

Mr. Coffee

Filters

■ **Filter broken cork from wine.** If you break the cork when opening a wine bottle, filter the wine through a Mr. Coffee Filter.

■ **Clean windows and mirrors.** Mr. Coffee Filters are lint-free, so they'll leave your windows sparkling.

■ **Protect china.** Separate your good dishes by putting a Mr. Coffee Filter between each dish.

■ **Cover bowls or dishes when cooking in the microwave.** Mr. Coffee Filters make excellent covers.

■ **Protect a cast-iron skillet.** Place a Mr. Coffee Filter in the skillet to absorb moisture and prevent rust.

■ **Apply shoe polish.** Ball up a lint-free Mr. Coffee Filter.

■ **Recycle frying oil.** After frying, strain oil through a sieve lined with a Mr. Coffee Filter.

■ **Weigh chopped foods.** Place chopped ingredients in a Mr. Coffee Filter on a kitchen scale.

■ **Hold tacos.** Mr. Coffee Filters make convenient wrappers for messy foods.

■ **Stop the soil from leaking out of a plant pot.** Line a plant pot with a Mr. Coffee Filter to prevent the soil from leaking through the drainage holes.

■ **Prevent a Popsicle from dripping.** Poke one or two holes as needed in a Mr. Coffee Filter, insert the Popsicle, and let the filter catch the drips.

Invented
1972

The Name
Inventor Vince Marotta, determined to give his coffeemaker a simple, catchy name, came up with Mr. Coffee off the top of his head.

A Short History
In the 1960s, Vince Marotta presided over North American Systems in Pepper Pike, OH, building shopping malls and housing developments. When business slowed in 1968,

Marotta fell ill, and while recuperating in bed, he realized how fed up he was with percolated coffee and decided to develop a better way to make coffee. He contacted the Pan American Coffee Bureau and discovered that South American coffee growers believed that the best way to extract the oil from coffee beans was to pour water, heated to 200°F, over the ground beans. Marotta hired engineer Irv Schultze to devise a bimetal actuator to control the temperature of the water. Observing how restaurants used a white cloth in their large coffee percolators to capture loose grounds and eliminate sediment, Marotta decided to use a paper filter in his coffeemaker.

Marotta showed up at the 1970 Housewares Convention in Chicago with a prototype for Mr. Coffee. On the spot, he hired Bill Howe, a buyer with Hamilton Beach, to represent his product. Howe invited 100 buyers up to Marotta's hotel room for coffee, and, within two years, Mr. Coffee was selling 42,000 coffee machines a day. According to Marotta, the paper filters—"the blade to the razor"—were cut and fluted by a paper company from an existing paper stock. Marotta sold the Mr. Coffee Company in 1987, and the company went public in 1990.

Ingredients
Virgin paper pulp

Strange Facts
■ In 1972, Marotta single-handedly convinced Joe DiMaggio to be the spokesman for Mr. Coffee's television commercials, which DiMaggio did for the next fifteen years.

■ Mr. Coffee machines outsell both Black & Decker and Proctor-Silex coffee machines by nearly two to one.

Distribution

■ Mr. Coffee is the best-selling coffeemaker in the world.
■ Since 1972, more than 50 million Mr. Coffee machines have been sold.
■ More than 10 billion Mr. Coffee paper filters are sold every year.

For More Information

Mr. Coffee, Inc., Bedford Heights, OH 44146. Or telephone 1-800-321-0370.

Morton Salt

■ **Soften a new pair of jeans.** Add one-half cup Morton Salt to detergent in the washing machine.

■ **Repel fleas.** Since salt repels fleas, wash doghouses with salt water to prevent fleas.

■ **Remove rust from household tools.** Make a paste using two tablespoons Morton Salt and one tablespoon ReaLemon. Apply the paste to rust with a dry cloth and rub.

■ **Dissolve soap suds in the sink.** Sprinkle Morton Salt on soap bubbles to make them pop.

■ **Clean coffee and tea stains from**

MORTON® SALT
HOUSEHOLD
HINT #9
See copy on
side panel

MORTON IODIZED SALT

THIS SALT SUPPLIES IODIDE, A NECESSARY NUTRIENT

china cups. Mix equal amounts Morton Salt and white vinegar.

■ Stop pipes from freezing or thaw frozen pipes.
Sprinkle Morton Salt down waste pipes in cold weather.

■ Clean dust off silk flowers. Put the flowers in a large paper bag, pour in two cups Morton salt, close the bag, and shake. Salt knocks the dust off the flowers. Remove the flowers from the bag and shake off the excess salt.

■ Remove dandruff. Shake one tablespoon Morton Salt into dry hair. Massage gently and shampoo.

■ Prevent grass from growing in crevices. Sprinkle Morton Salt in the cracks. Salt is a corrosive that kills plants.

■ Absorb spilled cooking grease or a broken egg.
Pour Morton Salt immediately on the spill, let sit for twenty minutes, then wipe up.

■ Prevent colors from fading in the wash. Add one cup coarse Morton Salt to detergent in the washing machine.

■ Keep slugs away. Sprinkle Morton Salt on the sidewalk close to the grass. When slugs try to approach your house, the salt will kill them by reverse osmosis. This works well in keeping slugs away from pet food, too.

Invented
1912

The Name

Morton Salt is named for company founders Joy and Mark Morton. An advertising agency developed the famous umbrella girl trademark, depicting a little girl standing in the rain with an umbrella over her head and holding a package of salt tilted backward with the spout open and the salt running out. In 1914, Joy Morton's son, Sterling Morton II, then president of the company, suggested the slogan "When It Rains It Pours" to convey the message that Morton Salt would pour easily even in damp weather.

A Short History

In 1879, Joy Morton, one of four sons born to J. Sterling Morton, acting governor of the Nebraska Territory, invested $10,000 to become a partner in E. I. Wheeler & Company, a Chicago company acting as an agent for Onondaga Salt. Following Wheeler's death in 1885, Morton acquired his partner's interest and, with his brother Mark, formed Joy Morton & Co., which soon became one of the largest producers of salt and the only nationwide salt company. In 1910, the partnership, which had acquired several other salt companies, became the Morton Salt Company. In 1912, Joy Morton developed Morton's Table Salt, a new, free-running salt packed in a blue-and-white cardboard canister with an aluminum pouring spout, invented by J. R. Harbeck.

Ingredients

Salt, sodium silicoaluminate, dextrose, potassium iodide

Strange Facts

■ The first written reference to salt is found in the story of Lot's wife, who was turned into a pillar of salt when she disobeyed the angels and looked back at Sodom.

■ The expression "He is not worth his salt" originated in ancient Greece, where salt was traded for slaves.

■ Roman soldiers were paid "salt money," salarium agentum, the origin of the English word salary.

■ The superstition that spilling salt brings bad luck may have its origins in Leonardo da Vinci's *Last Supper*, which depicts an overturned salt cellar in front of Judas Iscariot. The French believed that throwing a pinch of salt over the shoulder would hit the devil in the eye, preventing any further foul play.

■ The timeless Morton Umbrella Girl has been updated with new dresses and hairstyles five times since she first appeared in 1914. She was updated in 1921, 1933, 1941, 1956, and 1968.

■ Salt has an estimated 14,000 specific industrial applications, including general food seasoning, curing of animal hides, the preparation of saline solutions, the manufacture of chlorine gas (to make plastics, insecticides, synthetic fibers, and dyes), and the manufacture of sodium hydroxide (to make rayon, explosives, cosmetics, and pharmaceuticals).

■ Salt inhibits the growth of bacteria, yeast, and molds, working as a natural preservative in butter, margarine, salad dressings, sausages, cured meats, and various pickled products. Salt also plays a key role in the leavening of bread, the development of the texture and rind of natural cheeses, the bleached color of sauerkraut, and the tenderness of vegetables.

Distribution

■ In 1994, Morton International sold more than $541 million worth of salt worldwide, manufacturing an extensive line of Highway/Ice Control Salt, Grocery Salt, Water Conditioning Salt, Food/Chemical Processing Salt, and Agricultural Salt.

■ Morton International is the number one salt company in North America and the only nationally distributed salt in the United States.

For More Information

Morton International, Inc., Morton Salt, Chicago, IL 60606-1597. Or telephone 1-312-807-2000.

■ Soothe sunburn pain. Empty a jar of Nestea into a warm bath. Soak in the tea. The tannic acid will relieve the sunburn pain.

■ Clean a varnished floor, woodwork, or furniture. Cold Nestea makes an excellent cleaning agent for wood.

■ Remove corns. Soak the corn in warm Nestea for 30 minutes each day for a week or two until the tannic acid in the tea dissolves the corn.

■ Repair scratched woodwork. Mix one level teaspoon Nestea with two teaspoons water. Use a cotton ball to apply the paste to the scratched surface.

■ **Make a natural air freshener.** Mix one quart Nestea with four tablespoons lemon juice. Strain through a Mr. Coffee Filter. Pour into empty spray bottles.

■ **Tenderize meat.** Mix Nestea and use one part tea to one part double-strength beef stock as the liquid in a pot roast or stew. The tannin in the tea tenderizes meat.

Invented
1948

The Name
Nestea is an ingenious combination of the first syllable of the company name *Nestlé* (after company founder Henrí Nestlé) and the word tea. The German word *nestle* means "little nest," and the Nestlé logo was inspired from this meaning.

A Short History
In 1867, amid public concern over infant mortality, Henrí Nestlé of Vevey, Switzerland, developed Farine Lactée, an infant formula made from concentrated milk, sugar, and cereal. Eight years later Nestlé sold his company—then doing business in sixteen countries—for one million francs. In 1905, a year after the company began selling chocolate, Nestlé merged with the Anglo-Swiss Condensed Milk Company of central Switzerland under the Nestlé name. In 1938, Nestlé, then doing business with Brazilian coffee growers, introduced Nescafé instant coffee, which was distributed to American troops during World War II. That same year

Nestlé introduced the Nestlé Crunch bar, followed by Nestlé Quik drink mix in 1948 and Taster's Choice coffee in 1966.

The concept of iced tea, first introduced at the 1904 St. Louis World's Fair by a merchant trying to sell warm tea on a hot summer day (by simply pouring the tepid brew over ice), did not become popular until 1948, when Nestlé scientists introduced Nestea hot tea mix. In 1956, Nestlé scientists introduced Nestea iced tea mix, the first 100 percent instant tea soluble in both hot and cold water, popularized in television commercials with the slogan "Take the Nestea Plunge." Nestlé also owns L'Oréal, Libby's, Carnation, Hills Brothers, Vittel, Buitoni, Butterfinger, Baby Ruth, and more than 40 Stouffer's Hotels. In 1991, the Nestlé Beverage Company and the Coca-Cola Company formed Coca-Cola/Nestlé Refreshments Company to market ready-to-drink iced coffee, chocolate, and tea beverages worldwide.

Ingredients

100 percent tea

Strange Facts

■ Today, Nestlé is the largest packaged food manufacturer, coffee roaster, and chocolate maker in the world, operating 438 factories in 63 countries.

■ Nestlé is the largest company in Switzerland, yet more than 98 percent of its revenue comes from outside the country.

■ While tea is the world's most popular beverage, Americans consume more than 80 percent of their tea iced.

Events

The Tea Council of the United States has designated June "National Iced Tea Month."

Distribution

■ Americans currently drink nearly 35 billion glasses, or seven gallons per person, of iced tea every year, according to Nestea spokesperson Andrea Cook.

■ The full line of Nestea iced tea mix products includes Nestea Iced Tea Mix, Nestea 100 Percent Tea, Nestea 100 Percent Tea with Lemon, Nestea Sugarfree Iced Tea Mix, Nestea Ice Teasers, Nestea Tea Bags, Nestea Ready-to-Drink, and Nestea Instant Herb Teas.

For More Information

Nestlé Beverage Company, 345 Spear Street, San Francisco, CA 94105. Or telephone 1-800-637-8535.

Quaker Oats

■ **Relieve itching from chicken pox.** Pour one-half cup Quaker Oats in a blender and blend into a powder on medium-high speed, then sift. Put two tablespoons into a warm bath and soak in the oatmeal for 30 minutes.

■ **Give your hair a dry shampoo.** Apply dry Quaker Oats to your hair, work it through with your fingers, and brush it out to remove the oils.

■ **Give yourself a moisturizing facial.** Make a paste from Quaker Oats, lemon juice, and honey. Apply to face, let sit for ten minutes, then rinse with warm water.

Invented
1877

The Name
In 1887, Henry D. Seymour, one of the founders of a new American oatmeal milling company, purportedly came across an article on the Quakers in an encyclopedia and was struck by the similarity between the religious group's qualities and the image he desired for oatmeal. A second story contends that Seymour's partner, William Heston, an ancestor of Quakers, was walking in Cincinnati one day and saw a picture of

William Penn, the English Quaker, and was similarly struck by the parallels in quality.

A Short History

Oatmeal's popularity as a breakfast food soared when Ferdinand Schumacher, a German immigrant running a grocery store in Akron, OH, prepared oatmeal in such a way as to reduce cooking time, packing his prepared oatmeal in convenient glass jars. Schumacher's success inspired the launch of dozens of other oatmeal companies, including the Quaker Mill Company, founded in 1877 in Ravena, OH. Merchants bought oatmeal in nondescript barrels, selling it to customers by scooping it into brown paper bags. In 1880, Henry Crowell, president of the American Cereal Company, visualized the advantages of selling packaged products directly to consumers, packaging Quaker Oats in the now famous cardboard canister and launching an advertising campaign.

Ingredient
100 percent natural rolled oats

Strange Facts

■ The name Quaker Oats inspired several lawsuits. The Quakers themselves unsuccessfully petitioned the U.S. Congress to bar trademarks with religious connotations.

■ Explorer Robert Peary carried Quaker Oats to the North Pole, and explorer Admiral Richard Byrd carried Quaker Oats to the South Pole.

■ A gigantic likeness of the Quaker Oats man was placed on the White Cliffs of Dover in England, requiring an act of Parliament to have it removed.

■ In 1990, when the Quaker Oats Company used Popeye the Sailor Man in oatmeal ads, the Society of Friends objected, insisting that Popeye's reliance on physical violence is incompatible with the religion's pacifist principles. The Quaker Oats Company quickly apologized and ended the campaign.

■ In 1988, when nutritionists claimed that oat bran reduced cholesterol, sales for the Quaker Oats Company jumped 600 percent. In July 1992, a major report in the *Journal of the American Medical Association*, sponsored by the Quaker Oats Company, concluded that oat bran lowers blood cholesterol by an average of just 2 to 3 percent. On the bright side, the report claimed that a 1 percent reduction in cholesterol nationwide could lead to a 2 percent decrease in deaths from heart disease.

Distribution

■ In 1994, the Quaker Oats Company sold more than $403 million worth of hot cereals (Old Fashioned Quaker Oats, Quick Quaker Oats, and Instant Quaker Oatmeal), nearly six times its closest competitor, private-label brands.

■ Old Fashioned Quaker Oats and Quick Quaker Oats are the best-selling "long-cooking" cereals in the United States. ■ Instant Quaker Oatmeal is the best-selling "instant" hot cereal. In fact, Instant Quaker Oatmeal is the number three selling breakfast cereal in America.

■ Remove ink spots from cloth. While ink is wet, apply ReaLemon liberally to the spot, then wash garment in normal cycle with regular detergent in cold water.

■ Get rid of dandruff. Apply one tablespoon ReaLemon to your hair. Shampoo, then rinse with water. Rinse again with a mixture of two tablespoons ReaLemon with two cups water. Repeat every other day until dandruff disappears.

■ Write with invisible ink. Use a cotton swab as a pen to write in ReaLemon on a piece of white paper. Once it dries, hold the paper near a hot lightbulb. The writing will turn brown.

■ Eliminate blackheads. Apply some ReaLemon over blackheads before going to bed. Wait until morning to wash off the juice with cool water. Repeat for several nights until you see a big improvement in the skin.

■ Create blond highlights. Rinse your hair with one-quarter cup ReaLemon in three-quarters cup water.

■ Deodorize a cutting board. Wash with ReaLemon to rid a cutting board from the smell of garlic, onions, or fish.

■ Remove fruit or berry stains from your hands. Rinse hands with ReaLemon juice.

■ **Remove rust and the mineral discolorations from cotton T-shirts and briefs.** Use one cup ReaLemon in the washing machine.

■ **Clean a microwave oven.** Add four tablespoons ReaLemon to one cup water in a microwave-safe four-cup bowl. Boil for five minutes in the microwave, allowing the steam to condense on the inside walls of the oven. Then wipe clean.

■ **Whiten, brighten, and strengthen fingernails.** Soak fingernails in ReaLemon for ten minutes, brush with a mixture of equal parts white vinegar and warm water, then rinse well.

■ **Stop bleeding and disinfect minor wounds.** Pour ReaLemon on a cut or apply with a cotton ball.

■ **Relieve poison ivy.** Applying ReaLemon over the affected areas should soothe itching and alleviate the rash.

■ **Clear up facial blemishes.** Dab ReaLemon on the spot a few times a day.

■ **Eliminate odors in your humidifier.** Add four teaspoons ReaLemon to the water.

■ **Relieve rough hands or sore feet.** Apply ReaLemon, rinse, then massage with Star Olive Oil.

■ **Clean brass, copper, and stainless steel kitchen sinks.** Make a paste from ReaLemon and salt, scrub gently, then rinse with water.

■ **Relieve a cough.** Mix four tablespoons ReaLemon, one cup honey, and one-half cup Star Olive Oil. Heat five minutes, then stir vigorously for two minutes. Take one teaspoon every two hours.

■ **Train a dog to stop barking.** Squirt some ReaLemon in the dog's mouth and say "Quiet."

■ **Relieve constipation.** Before breakfast, drink four tablespoons ReaLemon in one cup warm water. Sweeten with honey.

Invented
Early 1940s

The Name
Company founder Irvin Swartzberg combined the words *real* and *lemon* and capitalized the shared letter *l* to form the clever hybrid ReaLemon.

A Short History
Irvin Swartzberg founded the Puritan-ReaLemon Company

in Chicago and began developing lemon juice products in 1934. His highly perishable products varied in strength and flavor because the lemons were not of uniform quality. In the early 1940s, after years of experimentation, Swartzberg produced a bottled lemon juice that was always consistent in flavor and strength by concentrating the juice of fresh lemons and then adding water. He also enhanced his product with filtration and preservation processes.

Ingredients

Water, lemon juice concentrate, lemon oil, .025 percent sodium benzoate (preservative) .025 percent sodium bisulfite (preservative)

Strange Facts

■ Three to four tablespoons ReaLemon equal the juice of one lemon.

■ Cutting down on sodium? Use ReaLemon instead of salt on vegetables, fish, chicken, pasta, or rice.

Distribution

■ ReaLemon is the best-selling lemon juice in the United States and the only nationally distributed brand of bottled lemon juice.

For More Information

Borden, Inc., Columbus, Ohio 43215. Or telephone 1-800-426-7336.

Reynolds Wrap

- **Remove rust spots from chrome car bumpers.** Rub the bumper with a crumpled-up piece of Reynolds Wrap dipped in Coca-Cola.

- **Keep dogs and cats off furniture.** Place pieces of Reynolds Wrap on the furniture. The sound of rustling foil frightens pets.

- **Clean pots and pans when camping.** A crumpled-up piece of Reynolds Wrap makes an excellent pot scrubber.

- **Fix battery-operated toys or appliances.** If the batteries in a Walkman or a toy are loose as the result of a broken spring, wedge a small piece of Reynolds Wrap between the battery and the spring.

- **Speed up your ironing.** Place a piece of aluminum foil under the ironing board cover to reflect the heat from the iron.

- **Make decorative trays or holiday decorations.** Cut cardboard into desired shape and size and cover with Reynolds Wrap.

- **Catch messy oven drips.** Tear off a sheet of Reynolds Wrap a few inches larger than baking pan. Place foil on the oven rack below the food being baked. (To prevent damage to the oven, do not use foil to line the bottom of the oven.)

■ **Avoid paint splatters.** Mold Reynolds Wrap around doorknobs when painting.

■ **Polish chrome.** Use a piece of crumpled-up Reynolds Wrap to polish the chrome on strollers, high chairs, and playpens.

■ **Improvise a funnel.** Double over a piece of Reynolds Wrap and roll into the shape of a cone.

■ **Secure plant cuttings.** Place Reynolds Wrap across the top of a glass jar filled with water. Poke holes in the foil and insert the cuttings securely in place. The foil also prevents the water from evaporating too quickly.

■ **Make a disposable palette.** Mix paints on a piece of Reynolds Wrap.

■ **Clean tarnished silverware.** Line a metal cake pan with Reynolds Wrap and fill with enough water to cover the silverware. Add two tablespoons baking soda per quart of water. Heat the water above 150°F. Place the tarnished silverware in the pan so it touches the aluminum foil. Do not let the water boil. The hydrogen from the baking soda combines with the sulfur in the tarnish, removing the stains.

■ **Clean a barbecue grill.** After barbecuing, place a sheet of Reynolds Wrap on the hot grill. The next time you use the barbecue, peel off the foil, crinkle it into a ball, and rub the grill clean, easily removing all the burned food.

■ **Re-adhere a linoleum floor tile.** Put a piece of Reynolds Wrap on top of the tile and run a hot iron over it several times to melt the glue underneath. Place several books on top of the tile until the glue dries completely.

■ **Prevent steel wool from rusting.** Wrap the pad in Reynolds Wrap and store it in the freezer.

■ **Clean starch off an iron.** Run the iron over a piece of Reynolds Wrap.

■ **Store wet paint brushes.** Wrap the wet brushes in Reynolds Wrap and store them in your freezer. When you're ready to paint again, defrost the brushes for an hour or more.

■ **Store leftover paint.** To prevent a layer of skin from forming over the paint surface, set the paint can on top of a sheet of Reynolds Wrap, trace around it, cut out a disc of foil, and place it on the paint surface before sealing the can closed.

Invented
.1947

The Name

Reynolds Wrap aluminum foil was named after the founder of Reynolds Metals Company, Richard S. Reynolds, Sr. The Reynolds logo, used since 1935, was inspired by Raphael's version of *St. George and the Dragon.* The legend of England's patron saint, depicted in several noted paintings, symbolizes the crusading spirit.

A Short History

Richard S. Reynolds worked for his uncle, tobacco king R. J. Reynolds, manufacturing the thin sheets of tin and lead foil then used to wrap cigarettes. In 1919, the young Reynolds started his own business, the U.S. Foil Co., supplying tin-lead wrappers to cigarette and candy companies. When the price of aluminum dropped in the 1920s, Reynolds switched to the new lightweight, noncorrosive metal. Reynolds Metals started producing aluminum siding, boats, cookware, and kitchen utensils. In 1947, Richard S. Reynolds introduced a .0007-inch-thick aluminum foil capable of conducting heat quickly and sealing in moisture.

Ingredients

Aluminum

Strange Facts

■ About 500 million pounds of aluminum foil and foil containers are used in the United States every year. That's equal to eight million miles of aluminum foil.

■ To recycle sheets of Reynolds Wrap aluminum foil used for cooking, simply rinse well to remove food particles. For the Reynolds Aluminum Recycling Center nearest you, call 1-800-344-WRAP.

Distribution

■ Reynolds Wrap can be found in three out of four American households.

■ As the only nationally distributed brand of aluminum foil, Reynolds Wrap is also the best-selling aluminum foil in America.

For More Information

Consumer Products Division, Reynolds Metals Company, Richmond, VA 23261. Or telephone 1-800-433-2244.

Silly Putty

- **Align and test CAT scanners.** Silly Putty's specific gravity is similar to human flesh.

- **Clean ink and ribbon fiber from typewriter keys.** Roll Silly Putty into a ball and press into the typewriter keys.

- **Collect cat fur and lint.** Flatten Silly Putty into a pancake and pat the surface.

- **Lift dirt from car seats.** Mold Silly Putty into whatever shape best fits into crevices.

- **Strengthen hands and forearm muscles.** Squeeze Silly Putty for ten minutes every day in each hand.

- **Fix a wobbly table.** Place a piece of Silly Putty under a leg.

- **Stop a small machine part from rattling.** Wrap Silly Putty as a buffer between two pieces of rattling metal.

■ **Calm your nerves.** Playing with Silly Putty has therapeutic value in reducing emotional pressure and calming nerves.

Invented
In the 1940s

The Name
Toy store proprietor and former advertising copywriter Paul Hodgson came up with the name Silly Putty off the top of his head while playing with the pink polymer.

A Short History
In the 1940s, when the United States War Production Board asked General Electric to synthesize a cheap substitute for rubber, James Wright, a company engineer assigned to the project in New Haven, CT, developed a pliant compound dubbed "nutty putty" with no real advantages over synthetic rubber. In 1949, Paul Hodgson, a former advertising copywriter running a New Haven toy store, happened to witness a demonstration of the "nutty putty" at a party. He bought 21 pounds of the putty for $147, hired a Yale student to separate it into half-ounce balls, and marketed the putty inside colored plastic eggs as Silly Putty. When it outsold every other item in his store, Hodgson mass-produced Silly Putty as "the toy with one moving part," selling up to 300 eggs a day. *The New Yorker* featured a short piece on Silly Putty in "Talk of the Town," launching an overnight novelty in the 1950s and 1960s.

Ingredients

Boric acid, silicone oil

Strange Facts

■ In 1961, Silly Putty attracted hundreds of Russians to the United States Plastics Expo in Moscow.

■ The astronauts on *Apollo 8* played with Silly Putty during their flight and used it to keep tools from floating around in zero gravity.

■ In 1981, the Columbus Zoo used Silly Putty to take hand- and footprints of gorillas for educational purposes.

■ Geology and astronomy professors often use Silly Putty to demonstrate the gradual movement of large masses of Earth.

■ Nonsmoking groups recommend Silly Putty to their members to give their hands something to do.

Distribution

■ Silly Putty was originally shipped in egg cartons purchased from the Connecticut Cooperative Poultry Association.

■ Americans buy over two million eggs of Silly Putty annually.

■ While the average fad lasts six months, demand for Silly Putty has surpassed 40 years.

■ Silly Putty comes in classic, glow-in-the-dark, glitter, and four hot fluorescent colors.

For More Information

Binney & Smith Inc., Easton, PA 18042-0431. Or telephone 1-800-272-9652.

Luncheon Meat

■ **Polish furniture.** SPAM purportedly makes good furniture polish, according to the *New York Times Magazine.*

■ **Steam-proof mirrors.** SPAM can be used to keep the condensation off the bathroom mirror when showering, also according to the *New York Times Magazine.*

■ **Go fishing.** SPAM makes excellent bait, according to Ann Kondo Corum, author of *Hawaii's* SPAM *Cookbook.*

Invented
1937

The Name

SPAM, possibly a contraction of *sp*iced h*am*, was named by actor Kenneth Daigneau, the brother of R. H. Daigneau, a former Hormel Foods vice president. When other meatpackers started introducing similar products, Jay C. Hormel decided to create a catchy brand name to give his spiced ham an unforgettable identity, offering a $100 prize to the person who came up with a new name. At a New Year's Eve party in 1936, Daigneau suggested the name SPAM.

A Short History

Jay C. Hormel, son of the company's founder, was determined to find a use for several thousand pounds of surplus pork shoulder. He developed a distinctive canned blend of chopped pork and ham known as Hormel spiced ham that didn't require refrigeration. SPAM luncheon meat was hailed as the "miracle meat," and its shelf-stable attributes attracted the attention of the United States military during World War II. By 1940, 70 percent of Americans  had tried it, and Hormel hired George Burns and Gracie Allen to advertise SPAM on their radio show. On March 22, 1994, Hormel Foods Corporation celebrated the production of its five billionth can of SPAM.

Ingredients

Chopped pork shoulder, chopped pork ham, salt, water, sugar, and sodium nitrate

Strange Facts

■ If laid end to end, five billion cans of SPAM would circle the earth 12.5 times.

■ Five billion cans of SPAM would feed a family of four three meals a day for 4,566,210 years.

■ One hundred million pounds of SPAM were issued as a Lend-Lease staple in the rations to American, Russian, and European troops during World War II, fueling the Normandy invasion. GIs called SPAM "ham that failed the physical." General Dwight D. Eisenhower confessed to "a few unkind words about it—uttered during the strain of battle."

■ Former British prime minister Margaret Thatcher, as a young woman of eighteen working in her family's grocery store, remembers SPAM as a "wartime delicacy."

■ In *Khrushchev Remembers*, Nikita Khrushchev credited SPAM with keeping the Russian Army alive during World War II. "We had lost our most fertile, food-bearing lands—the Ukraine and the Northern Caucasians. Without SPAM, we wouldn't have been able to feed our army."

■ In the 1980s, David Letterman suggested SPAM-on-a-Rope for his *Late Night* audience "in case you get hungry in the shower."

■ When Vernon Tejas made his solo winter ascent of Mount McKinley in 1988, he took a picture of himself with a can of SPAM at the summit.

■ Hormel Foods board chairman R. L. Knowlton presented a can of SPAM to Mikhail Gorbachev in June 1990 and another can of SPAM to Boris Yeltsin in June 1992.

■ The Pentagon sent approximately $2 million worth of SPAM to United States troops during the Gulf war.

■ South Koreans consider SPAM an upscale food. The *Wall*

Street Journal reported that a Seoul executive in search of the perfect present bought SPAM, explaining, "It is an impressive gift."

■ Anthropologist Jane Goodall and her mother once made 2,000 SPAM sandwiches for Belgian troops fleeing from their African colony.

Recipes

■ SPAM can be grilled, panfried, broiled, sautéed, and baked or added to ethnic dishes, sandwiches, pasta salads, pizzas, casseroles, stir-fry dishes, appetizers, and soups.

■ The Ala Moana Poi Bow in Honolulu serves SPAM musubi and SPAM, eggs, and rice.

■ The Green Midget Cafe, created by Monty Python's Flying Circus, serves "egg and SPAM; egg, bacon, and SPAM; egg, bacon, sausage, and SPAM; SPAM, bacon, sausage, and SPAM; SPAM, egg, SPAM, SPAM, bacon, and SPAM; SPAM, SPAM, SPAM, egg, and SPAM; SPAM, SPAM, SPAM, SPAM, SPAM, SPAM, baked beans, SPAM, SPAM, SPAM, and SPAM; or lobster thermidor aux crevettes with a Mornay sauce garnished with truffle pâté, brandy, and a fried egg on top and SPAM."

■ Mr. Whitekeys' Fly by Night Club in Spenard, AK, offers Cajun SPAM, SPAM nachos, and pasta with SPAM and sundried tomatoes in cream sauce.

■ The winning recipes from the 1992 State Fair Best of SPAM Recipe Competition included SPAM Mousse, SPAM Golden Harvest Corn Chowder, and SPAM Cheesecake.

■ A SPAMBURGER, "the only hamburger actually made with ham," can be made by grilling, panfrying, or broiling a slice of SPAM and then layering the slice with lettuce, tomato, mayonnaise, and cheese on a hamburger bun.

■ Hormel Foods' cookbook, *The Great Taste of* SPAM, includes recipes for SPAM Stew with Buttermilk Topping, SPAM Fajitas, and SPAM Strudels with Mustard Sauce.

Unusual Events

■ Sixty-eight state and regional fairs hold Hormel Foods–sanctioned SPAM recipe contests each year.

■ In Hawaii, Maui Mall hosts an annual SPAM cook-off.

■ Austin, TX, has been home to the SPAMorama barbecue and cooking contest since 1974.

■ Seattle, WA, hosts a yearly SPAM luncheon meat celebration.

■ The SPAM Jamboree, held every Fourth of July weekend in Austin, MN, is the only SPAM event Hormel officially sponsors.

■ At the 1983 SPAMposium, 33 self-proclaimed SPAMophiles gathered from across the nation to deliver scholarly papers and demonstrations, including making explosives from SPAM.

Distribution

■ Americans consume 113 million cans of SPAM a year.

■ The average Hawaiian eats twelve cans of SPAM a year, followed by the average Alaskan with six cans, and then Texans, Alabamians, and Arkansans with three cans apiece.

For More Information

Hormel Foods Corporation, 1 Hormel Place, Austin, MN 55912-3680. Or telephone 1-800-523-4635.

Star

Olive Oil

■ **Shave.** If you run out of shaving cream, slather on Star Olive Oil.

■ **Slow a dog from shedding.** Pour one table-spoon Star Olive Oil on your dog's food while the dog is shedding.

■ **Clean pearls.** Rub a dab of Star Olive Oil over pearls, cleaning each pearl individually. Wipe dry with a chamois cloth.

■ **Polish lacquered metal.** Use a few drops of Star Olive Oil on a soft cloth.

■ **Relieve a cough.** Mix three to four tablespoons lemon juice, one cup honey, and one-half cup Star Olive Oil. Heat for five minutes, then stir vigorously for two minutes. Take one teaspoon every two hours.

■ **Soothe frostbite.** Warm some Star Olive Oil and gently dab on frostbitten skin.

■ **Relieve a scalded throat.** Take two teaspoons Star Olive Oil to coat and soothe the throat.

■ **Rejuvenate dry skin.** Lubricate with Star Olive Oil.

■ **Condition your hair.** Warm up Star Olive Oil, massage it into your hair and scalp, wrap your head in a towel, and sit under a dryer. Later, shampoo as usual.

■ **Relieve jellyfish or man-of-war stings.** Apply Star Olive Oil for immediate relief, then seek medical attention.

■ **Soothe an earache.** Warm and insert a few drops Star Olive Oil into the affected ear, plug with cotton, and apply a hot water bottle.

■ **Relieve bursitis.** Heat Star Olive Oil and massage into the shoulder or upper arm daily.

■ **Rejuvenate a palm or fern plant.** Add two tablespoons Star Olive Oil at the root of the plant once a month.

■ **Relieve constipation.** Take one to three tablespoons Star Olive Oil as a mild laxative.

Invented

3300 B.C.

The Name

Olive oil is the oil squeezed from an olive. Company founder Angelo Giurlani originally gave his olives the brand name *Stella*, the Italian word for *star*, but later changed the name to Star to give the company a more American flavor and increase sales.

A Short History

Olive oil is a fragrant, edible oil obtained by pressing and crushing fresh olives. As early as 3300 B.C., villages on the Aegean islands were trading olive oil with the Greek mainland and Crete. Today, Italy is the world's leading producer of olive oil, followed by Spain and Greece. In 1898, Angelo Giurlani and his brothers, all Italian immigrants, founded A. Giurlani & Bro. Inc., to import, pack, and distribute olive oil. In 1987, the company changed its name to Giurlani USA.

Ingredients

100 percent olive oil

Strange Facts

■ Olive Oyl is the name of Popeye the Sailor Man's girlfriend.

■ According to the Talmud, around 165 B.C.E. a small jar of olive oil burned in the temple of Jerusalem for eight days, astonishing the Maccabees (the Jewish army that had just recaptured the city from the Syrians). The Jewish holiday of Chanukah celebrates that wonder.

■ In ancient Egypt and Greece, women were advised to insert olive oil into their vaginas for contraceptive purposes. Olive oil was thought to prevent sperm from entering the uterus. It doesn't.

Distribution

■ Star Olive Oil is available in Original and Extra Light in Flavor.

■ Star also imports, packs, and distributes Spanish olives, wine vinegars, capers, cocktail onions, specialty peppers, sun dried tomatoes, anchovies, and maraschino cherries.

For More Information

Giurlani USA, 4652 East Date Avenue, Fresno, CA 93725. Or telephone 1-209-498-2900.

Tidy Cat

■ **Create emergency traction for automobiles.** Keep a bag of Tidy Cat in your car trunk in case you get stuck in the ice or snow. When poured under the tire, it provides excellent traction.

■ **Soak up car oil and transmission fluid.** Tidy Cat works as an absorbent to pick up transmission leaks from garage floors. Pour a thick layer of unused Tidy Cat over the puddle, wait 24 hours, and sweep up with a broom. Scrub clean with a solution of detergent and hot water.

■ **Deodorize a garbage can.** Cover bottom of garbage can with one inch unused Tidy Cat to absorb grease and moisture.

■ **Prevent mildew in bathtub.** Pour unused Tidy Cat in a flat box and place in your bathtub to prevent mildew when you leave your house for a long time. (Keep the bathroom door closed if you have cats so they don't use it.)

■ **Deodorize a stale refrigerator.** Pour unused Tidy Cat in a flat box, place it on the middle shelf, and shut the door for five days.

■ **Provide traction on snow-covered driveways and sidewalks.** Sprinkle unused Tidy Cat on the snow-covered walk.

■ **Prevent musty, damp odors in a closed summer house.** Fill shallow boxes with unused Tidy Cat. To soak up musty, lingering odors, place one in each room before closing up the house.

■ **Deodorize sneakers.** Fill the feet of knee high hose with unused Tidy Cat, tie the ends, and place inside sneakers overnight.

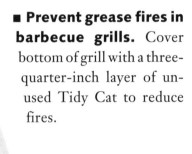

■ **Prevent grease fires in barbecue grills.** Cover bottom of grill with a three-quarter-inch layer of unused Tidy Cat to reduce fires.

Invented
1971

The Name

Ed Lowe coined the name Kitty Litter® and sold his first cat box filler exclusively through pet stores beginning in 1947. Twenty years later, when grocery stores finally agreed to carry Kitty Litter,

Lowe repackaged his product as Tidy Cat (so the grocery stores could charge a lower price for the cat box filler while the pet stores could continue charging a premium price for Kitty Litter). Lowe came up with the name Tidy Cat from the way Kitty Litter helps keep a cat box tidy.

A Short History

In 1947, Edward Lowe went into business with his father and one employee to supply sawdust and absorbent clay to local Michigan and northern Indiana industries, including Bendix, Whirlpool, and Studebaker. In the winter of 1947, Ed Lowe's clay was first used as cat box filler with the introduction of Kitty Litter Brand, sold through pet stores. In 1971, Lowe introduced Tidy Cat for exclusive sale through grocery stores, creating the first nationally advertised cat box filler. In 1977, Lowe introduced the first microencapsulated deodorant system, followed by the first dual-deodorant system in 1985 and the first cat box filler that fights odor-causing bacteria in 1989.

Ingredients

Ground clay, deodorizing system, baking soda

Strange Facts

■ Tidy Cat reacts to the pH level of cat urine but is also sensitive to the presence of ammonia odors.

■ Ed Lowe's autobiography, *Tail of the Entrepreneur*, published in 1994, tells the inspiring story of the Kitty Litter empire.

■ A parasite sometimes found in cat feces can cause toxoplasmosis in pregnant women and those with suppressed immune systems. Special care should be taken in handling used cat box filler. Keep box away from food preparation areas and wash hands thoroughly after handling to reduce risk of infection. For more information, consult your physician.

Distribution

■ Tidy Cat ranks as the best-selling cat box filler in the United States.

For More Information

Golden Cat Corporation, P.O. Box 1958, Cape Girardeau, MO 63702-1958. Or telephone 1-800-835-6369.

Petroleum Jelly

■ **Lure trout.** Coat small pieces of sponge with Vaseline petroleum jelly to simulate fish-egg bait.

■ **Prevent car battery corrosion.** Smear Vaseline petroleum jelly on clean car battery terminals.

■ **Repair stains, rings, and minor scratches in wood furniture.** Cover each scratch with a liberal coat of Vaseline petroleum jelly, let sit for 24 hours, rub into wood, wipe away excess, and polish as usual.

■ **Remove chewing gum from hair.** Apply Vaseline petroleum jelly and work into hair until gum slides off.

■ **Stop a faucet from screeching.** Remove the handle and stem, coat both sets of metal threads with Vaseline petroleum jelly, and replace.

■ **Lubricate roller skate and skateboard wheels.** Smear Vaseline petroleum jelly around the cylinders on the wheels so they roll faster.

■ **Remove a ring stuck on a finger.** Coat finger with Vaseline petroleum jelly and slide the ring off.

■ **Moisturize your face.** Wash your face thoroughly and,

while still wet, rub in a small dab of Vaseline petroleum jelly. Keep wetting face until the Vaseline petroleum jelly is spread evenly and does not appear greasy. Health spas use this secret treatment.

■ **Revive dried leather.** Vaseline petroleum jelly, rubbed into a baseball glove, softens the leather.

■ **Prevent rust on outdoor machinery.** Apply a generous coat of Vaseline petroleum jelly.

■ **Avoid splattered paint on windows, metalwork, and floors.** Before painting a room, dip a cotton swab in Vaseline petroleum jelly and run it around the edges of the glass; coat door hinges, doorknobs, lock latches; and spread a thin coat of Vaseline petroleum jelly along a linoleum or tile floor (obviously not carpet) where it meets the wall. Paint smears will wipe off with a cloth.

■ **Remove makeup.** Vaseline petroleum jelly takes off mascara, eyeliner, lipstick, rouge, and powders.

■ **Prevent the cap from sticking shut on nail polish bottles.** Put a thin coat of Vaseline petroleum jelly around the rim of the bottle.

■ **Keep shower curtains sliding easily.** Apply a thin coat of Vaseline petroleum jelly to the curtain rod.

■ **Prevent a sailboat's spinnaker pole fittings from jamming or sticking.** Lubricate with Vaseline petroleum jelly.

■ **Help prevent diaper rash.** Apply a thin coat of Vaseline petroleum jelly to a baby's clean bottom before putting a fresh diaper on the infant.

■ **Prevent outdoor lightbulbs from sticking in fixtures.** To make removal easy, rub a thin coat of Vaseline petroleum jelly on the threads before inserting the bulbs.

■ **Heal chapped lips.** Apply a little Vaseline petroleum jelly to the lips before going outdoors and again before going to bed.

■ **Remove lipstick stains from linen napkins.** Apply Vaseline petroleum jelly before washing.

■ **Prevent hair coloring from dying your skin.** Rub Vaseline petroleum jelly along hairline before coloring your hair.

■ **Protect skin from windburn and chapping.** Apply a thin coat of Vaseline petroleum jelly.

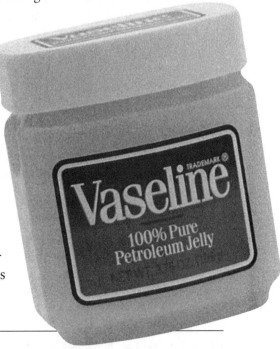

■ **Stop refrigerator racks from sticking.** Coat the edges of the racks with Vaseline petroleum jelly so the racks glide easily.

■ **Discourage candle wax from sticking to candle-holders.** Coat the insides of candleholders with Vaseline petroleum jelly so wax slides out.

■ **Keep shampoo from getting in a baby's eyes.** Rub a line of Vaseline petroleum jelly above the eyebrows so shampoo runs off to the side.

■ **Shine leather shoes.** Rub Vaseline petroleum jelly over the leather and wipe off the excess with a towel.

Invented
1887

The Name
Vaseline inventor Robert Augustus Chesebrough combined the German word *wasser* (water) with the Greek word *elaion* (olive oil).

A Short History
In 1859, Robert Augustus Chesebrough, a Brooklyn chemist whose kerosene business faced impending closure, traveled to Titusville, PA, to enter the competing petroleum business. Intrigued by the jelly residue that gunked up drilling rods, Chesebrough learned from workers that the jelly quickened healing when rubbed on a wound or burn. Chesebrough brought jars of the whipped gunk back to Brooklyn, where he purified the petroleum lard into a clear, smooth gel he called "petroleum jelly" and started manufacturing Vaseline in 1887.

Ingredients

White petrolatum, USP

Strange Facts

- Explorer Robert Peary brought Vaseline petroleum jelly to the North Pole to protect his skin from chapping and his mechanical equipment from rusting.

- Since petroleum jelly withstands tropical climates, Amazonian natives cooked with Vaseline petroleum jelly and ate it on bread.

- Cosmetic manufacturers buy Vaseline petroleum jelly in bulk as a base for beauty creams. Pharmaceutical companies use Vaseline petroleum jelly as a base to create their own brands of salves and creams. Before Vaseline petroleum jelly, pharmacists used a base of lard or glycerin (animal or vegetable matter), which quickly decomposed and became rancid.

- Sales of Vaseline petroleum jelly soared in Russia in 1916 when peasants discovered that adding the petroleum jelly to the oil burned in their holy lamps eliminated the choking smoke fumes.

- Sales of Vaseline petroleum jelly soared in China with Sun Yat-sen's liberation of the Chinese people in 1917. Coolies, ordered to clip off their pigtails (a mark of subjugation), discovered that Vaseline petroleum jelly eased the discomfort caused by the bristle of the severed pigtail.

- Talking Heads' greatest hits album is titled *Sand in the Vaseline.*

Distribution

■ A jar of Vaseline petroleum jelly can be found in virtually every home in the United States.

■ Chesebrough-Ponds manufactures Vaseline petroleum jelly, Medicated Vaseline petroleum jelly, Vaseline Intensive Care Lotion, and Vaseline Lip Therapy (for chapped lips).

For More Information

Chesebrough-Ponds USA, Greenwich, CT 06830. Or telephone 1-800-743-8640.

■ **Attract fish.** When sprayed on fishing bait, WD-40 covers up the scent of human hands on the bait to better lure fish, according to *USA Today*. The WD-40 Company receives hundreds of letters from consumers confirming this use but prefers not to promote WD-40 as a fishing lure because the petroleum-based product could potentially pollute rivers and streams, damaging the ecosystem.

■ **Cure mange.** While spraying a dog with WD-40 gets rid of parasitic mites, according to *USA Today*, the WD-40 Company, feeling that the potential misuse of the product is too great, refuses to condone using WD-40 to cure mange on animals.

■ **Prevent squirrels from climbing into a birdhouse.** Spray WD-40 on the metal pole or wires.

■ **Remove a ring stuck on a finger.** Several medical journals claim that WD-40 is the perfect cure for a toe stuck in the bathtub faucet, a finger stuck in a soda bottle, or a ring stuck on a finger.

■ **Clean decorative snow from windows.** Spray windows with WD- 40 before spraying with artificial snow so the decorative spray will wipe off easier.

■ **Prevent dead insects from sticking to your car.** Spray WD-40 on the hood and grille so you can wipe bugs off easily without damaging the finish.

■ **Remove chewing gum, crayon, tar, and Silly Putty from most surfaces.** Spray on WD-40, wait, and wipe.

■ **Make hangers glide over a clothes rod.** Spray WD-40 on the clothes rod so hangers can be pushed back and forth easily.

■ **Clean clogged spray-paint-can nozzles.** Remove the nozzles from the spray-paint can and the WD-40 can, place the nozzle from the spray-paint can on the WD-40 can, give it a couple of quick squirts, and replace both nozzles.

■ **Remove oil spots from driveways.** Spray with WD-40, wait, then blot. The mineral spirits and other petroleum distillates in WD-40 work as a curing agent.

■ **Thread electrical wire through conduits.** Spray WD-40 on electrical wire to help it glide through winding conduits.

■ **Prevent grass clippings from clogging up a lawn mower.** Spray WD-40 on the underside of the lawn mower housing and blade before cutting the grass.

■ **Clean sap from gardening equipment.** Spray with WD-40, wait, and wipe clean.

■ **Prevent mud and clay buildup on bicycles.** Spray the bicycle with a thin coat of WD-40.

■ **Remove baked-on food from a cookie pan.** Spray WD-40 on cookie pan and wipe clean. Then wash with soap and water.

■ **Remove dirt and grime from barbecue grills.** Remove the grill from the barbecue, spray with WD-40, wait, and wipe clean. Then wash with soap and water.

■ **Remove chewing gum from the bottom of a shoe or sneaker.** Spray on WD-40, wait, and pull the gum free.

■ **Keep dogs, maggots, and flies out of trash cans.** Coat the trash cans with a thin layer of WD-40.

■ **Take squeaks out of new shoes.** Spray WD-40 into the leather and shine.

■ **Remove grease stains from linen.** Spray WD-40 directly to the stain, rub it in, let soak for a few minutes, then wash through a regular cycle.

■ **Take squeaks out of a box-spring mattress.** Remove the fabric covering the bottom of the box-spring mattress (simply by removing the staples) and spray the springs with WD-40. Staple the fabric back in place with a staple gun.

■ **Polish wood furniture.** Spray WD-40 on a cloth and wipe.

■ **Clean crayon from a blackboard.** Spray WD-40 on the crayon marks, let soak for ten minutes, then blot clean with a cloth.

■ **Free a tongue stuck to frozen metal.** Spray WD-40 on the metal around the tongue.

Invented

1953

Name

Norman Larsen, president and head chemist at the Rocket Chemical Company, developed a *w*ater *d*isplacement formula on his 40th try, naming it WD-40.

A Short History

The aerospace industry needed a product to eliminate moisture from electrical circuitry and to prevent corrosion on airplanes and Atlas Missile nosecones. The newly developed WD-40 worked so well, engineers working at the Rocket Chemical Company began sneaking it out of the plant for home use on squeaky doors and stuck locks. WD-40 became available to the public in 1958, and in 1961, a sweet fragrance was added to overcome the smell of the petroleum distillates. In 1969, the Rocket Chemical Company was renamed the WD-40 Company, after its only product. The WD-40 Company makes the "secret sauce," then sends it to packagers who add the solvent and propellant.

Ingredients
Petroleum distillates, fragrance

Strange Facts
■ In 1964, John Glenn circled the earth in *Friendship VII*, which was covered with WD-40 from top to bottom.
■ The WD-40 Company went public on the NASDAQ exchange in 1973. The initial 300,000 shares, available at $16.50, closed that same day at $26.50.
■ WD-40 makes more than a million gallons of the "secret sauce" every year.

Distribution
■ WD-40 can be found in four out of five American homes. It is distributed to 115 countries around the world.
■ Worldwide sales of WD-40 in 1994 were $112 million.

For More Information
WD-40 Company, P.O. Box 80607, San Diego, CA 92138-0607. Or telephone 1-619-275-1400.

Worcestershire Sauce

■ **Remove tarnish from copper pots.** With a soft cloth, rub Worcestershire Sauce on the tarnish.

■ **Polish brass.** Apply Worcestershire Sauce with a damp cloth.

■ **Repair scratched woodwork or furniture.** Use a cotton ball to apply Worcestershire Sauce to the scratched surface.

Invented
1835

The Name
Worcestershire Sauce was named for the town of Worcester, England, which is in the shire (county) of Worcester.

A Short History
In 1835, when Lord Marcus Sandys, governor of Bengal, retired to Ombersley, England,

he longed for his favorite Indian sauce. He took the recipe to a drugstore on Broad Street in nearby Worcester, where he commissioned the shopkeepers, John Lea and William Perrins, to mix up a batch. Lea and Perrins made a large batch, hoping to sell the excess to other customers. The pungent fishy concoction wound up in the cellar, where it sat undisturbed until Lea and Perrins rediscovered it two years later when housecleaning. Upon tasting the aged sauce, Lea and Perrins bottled Worcestershire sauce as a local dip. When Lea and Perrins's salesmen convinced British passenger ships to put the sauce on their dining room tables, Worcestershire Sauce became an established steak sauce across Europe and the United States.

Ingredients

Water, vinegar, molasses, high fructose corn syrup, anchovies, hydrolyted soy and corn protein, onions, tamarinds, salt, garlic, cloves, chili peppers, natural flavorings, and échalotes

Strange Facts

■ To this day, the ingredients in Worcestershire Sauce are stirred together and allowed to sit for up to two years before being bottled.

■ An advertisement in 1919 falsely claimed that Worcestershire sauce was "a wonderful liquid tonic that makes your hair grow beautiful."

■ In a famous photograph taken on September 30, 1938, of Neville Chamberlain having dinner with Adolf Hitler, Benito Mussolini, and Edouard Daladier, a bottle of Lea & Perrins Worcestershire Sauce sits on the table.

Distribution

■ Lea & Perrins Worcestershire Sauce is the best-selling dark Worcestershire sauce in the world.

For More Information

Lea & Perrins, Inc., Fair Lawn, NJ 07410. Or telephone 1-201-791-1600.

Storage Bags

■ **Keep passports waterproof.** Store your passport in a Ziploc Storage Bag.

■ **Protect important papers.** Store tax forms, important records, canceled checks, receipts, warranties, and instructions in a Ziploc Storage Bag.

■ **Store camping items.** Carry utensils, food, clothes, maps, medications, and first aid supplies in Ziploc Storage Bags.

■ **Carry a wet sponge or cloth for sticky fingers.** Travel with your own dampened wipe in a Ziploc Storage Bag.

■ **Separate lingerie, scarves, gloves, hosiery, and handkerchiefs.** Organize your smaller garments in Ziploc Storage Bags.

■ **Keep jewelry together.** Organize rings, earrings, necklaces, and brooches in Ziploc Storage Bags.

■ **Improvise a diaper changing mat.** In an emergency, a jumbo Ziploc Storage Bag can be used as an easy-to-tote changing mat.

■ **Carry dirty diapers in a baby bag without any offending odors.** Keep extra Ziploc Storage Bags in your baby bag so you can seal dirty diapers until you can dispose of them properly. This is especially considerate when visiting friends' homes.

■ **Carry snacks.** When traveling, pack snacks in Ziploc Storage Bags.

■ **Carry a change of baby clothes.** Pack a change of clothes for a baby in a Ziploc Storage Bag. In separate bags, store a pacifier, cotton balls, and medication. Place all the items in a jumbo zippered Storage Bag and keep it in the baby bag.

■ **Pack toiletries when you travel.** Keep all your toiletry items together in a Ziploc Storage Bag and prevent any unexpected leaks or spills.

■ **Store game pieces.** Never lose dice, cards, playing pieces, or small toys again.

■ **Pack seasonal items away.** Store leftover holiday greeting cards, valentines, and Halloween decorations in Ziploc Storage Bags.

■ **Pack a child's suitcase with ease.** Organize your children's outfits in jumbo Ziploc Storage Bags. Put a matching top, bottom, a pair of underwear and socks in each bag so kids know exactly what they're going to wear each day of a vacation.

■ **Marinate meats.** Combine your food marinate ingredients in a Ziploc Storage Bag, and refrigerate.

■ **Store crayons.** Keep a few crayons in a Ziploc Storage Bag for trips so kids always have something to do in restaurants or while traveling.

■ **Store leftovers.** Keep leftovers for single servings in Ziploc Storage Bags for quick meals.

■ **Organize store coupons.** Keep coupons in Ziploc Storage Bags for easy reference.

■ **Make potpourri.** Collect dried roses, juniper sprigs, tiny pinecones, strips of orange rind, bay leaves, cinnamon sticks, whole cloves, and allspice berries. Mix a few drops of rose, cinnamon, and balsam oils with orrisroot (available at your local crafts store). Add all ingredients and seal in a Ziploc Storage Bag for a few weeks to mellow, turning the bag occasionally.

■ **Store jigsaw puzzles.** Keep all the pieces in a Ziploc

Storage Bag so you never lose that one pivotal piece of the puzzle again.

■ **Store screws, nuts, and bolts.** Organize nuts, bolts, drill bits, nails, washers, and screws in the workshop.

■ **Store crafts.** Organize paintbrushes, ribbons, beads, glues, and strings in Ziploc Storage Bags.

■ **Store leftover garden seeds.** Seal seeds and put them in a cool, dry place until ready for planting.

■ **Pipe icing on a cake.** Fill a pint-size Ziploc Storage Bag with icing, twist the bag to force icing to one corner, seal, and use scissors to snip a small bit off the corner. Squeeze out icing to make polka dots or squiggles or to write names. Use a separate bag for each color.

■ **Clean a showerhead.** If a showerhead cannot be removed for cleaning, fill a Ziploc bag with vinegar, wrap it around the showerhead, and secure in place overnight with a rubber band.

Invented
1970

The Name
Ziploc is a clever hybrid of the words *zipper* and *lock*—a mnemonic device to remind consumers that the bags zip shut and lock tight.

A Short History

Herbert H. Dow founded the Dow Chemical Company with the discovery of salt deposits in northern Michigan, expanding into the research, development, and manufacture of industrial chemicals. Dow started manufacturing consumer products in 1953 with the introduction of Saran Wrap, followed by Handi-Wrap in 1960, Dow Oven Cleaner in 1963, and Scrubbing Bubbles in 1966. In 1970, Dow unveiled the Ziploc Storage Bag with its patented tongue-in-groove "Gripper Zipper," providing a virtually airtight, watertight seal that revolutionized plastic bags.

Ingredient

Polyethylene

Strange Facts

■ Ziploc Storage Bags were the first food storage bag with the zipperlike seal available to consumers.

■ Consumers rate Ziploc Storage Bags as the easiest bags to close.

■ Ziploc Brand Bags are recyclable under the plastic recycling number 4, although, as of this writing, it is difficult to find a local recycling center able to recycle this type of plastic.

■ Ziploc Storage Bags may be used for microwave reheating, and Ziploc Freezer Bags may be used for microwave reheating and defrosting. Vent the zipper one inch to allow steam to escape, and use the reheat or defrost setting only for a short amount of time. Do not microwave foods high in sugar or fat in a Ziploc Storage Bag; foods high in sugar or fat content respond quickly to microwave energy and may melt the bag. Ziploc Sandwich Bags should not be used in the microwave because they are too thin.

■ Do not boil food in Ziploc brand bags. The bags will soften at 195°F, which is below the temperature of boiling water.

Distribution

■ DowBrands manufactures Ziploc Storage Bags, Ziploc Freezer Bags, Ziploc Sandwich Bags, Ziploc Vegetable Bags, and Ziploc Snack Bags.

For More Information

DowBrands L.P., P.O. Box 68511, Indianapolis, IN 46268-0511. Or telephone 1-800-428-4795.

Dawn®

Kill insects on plant leaves. Mix one-half cup Dawn dishwashing detergent to one pint water. Spray on both sides of plant leaves, let sit for one hour, then spray clean with water. **For More Information:** Procter & Gamble, Cincinnati, OH 45202. Or telephone 1-800-725-DAWN.

Liquid Paper®

Camouflage stained grout. Simply paint the grout with Liquid Paper. **Cover up scuff marks on white shoes.** Touch up with Liquid Paper. **For More Information:** The Gillette Company, Stationery Products Division, Box 61, Boston, MA 02199. Or telephone 1-800-884-4443.

Pampers®

Control heavy bleeding. Use a pair of Pampers as a compress. **For More Information:** Procter & Gamble, Cincinnati, OH 45202. Or telephone 1-800-285-6064.

Tampax® Tampons

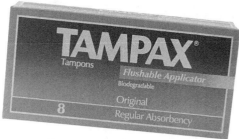

Control heavy bleeding. A tampon can be used as a compress for wounds or lacerations. **For More Information:** Tambrands Inc., Palmer, MA 01069. Or telephone 1-800-523-0014.

If you know more offbeat uses for brand-name products, send your tips and suggestions to:
Joey Green
Polish Your Furniture with Panty Hose
c/o Hyperion
114 Fifth Avenue
New York, NY 10011

Acknowledgments

If not for my extraordinary editor, Laurie Abkemeier, this quirky manifesto would be a pile of yellowing papers in a box in the back of my closet. Her enthusiasm, passion, and keen sense of humor made working on this book a joy.

At Hyperion, I am grateful to Bob Miller, Adrian James, Mark Rifkin, Claudyne Bianco, and the flotilla of copyeditors and proofreaders who gave their lives for this book.

No amount of thanks can properly express my appreciation to my agent, Jeremy Solomon, for his astounding professionalism, incredible drive, and entrepreneurial savvy.

In the corporate world, I am indebted to Mary Jon Dunham and Melinda Bollenbacher at Procter & Gamble (makers of Bounce, Ivory soap, Jif, Dawn, and Pampers), Melissa Minsky and Peter Sanders at Clairol (makers of Herbal Essences), Norman Mandel at the Coca-Cola Company, Patrick Boland and Joanne Feeney at Colgate-Palmolive, Meghan Flynn at Burson/Marsteller (public relations firm for Dannon), John O'Shea, Sally Dancos, and Sharon Meckes at Warner-Lambert (makers of Efferdent and Listerine), John A. Jones, Kelly Rae Cooper, and Jerome R. Schindler at Borden (makers of Elmer's Glue-All), Nancy Lovre at Beecham, Inc. (makers of Geritol), Scott Thayer, Valerie Sciotto, and Ed Gleason at Heinz U.S.A., Sandra Davenport at the Vinegar Institute, Michael Mazza, Sandy Sullivan, and Trish Cetrone at the Clorox Company (makers of Kingsford Charcoal Briquets), Arthur DeBaugh, Kevin

Mundy, and James Friedan at Sara Lee (makers of L'eggs), Daniel Gross at J. Walter Thompson (advertising agency for Listerine), Gary Wilkerson and Amy Fuelling at Maybelline, Danielle Taylor and Janine Kober at Lippe Taylor (public relations for Maybelline), Dan Carlson, Kathy Vanderwist, and Steve Flint at Mr. Coffee, Vince Marotta (founder of Mr. Coffee), Nancy Hober and Robert Didrick at Morton International, Robert Collins, Rich M. Gacer, and Jennifer Sievers at Nestlé, Janet Silverberg at the Quaker Oats Company, Alan McDonald and Carol Owen at Reynolds Metals, Sylvia Woolf Gallop at Binney & Smith (makers of Silly Putty), Kevin Jones at Hormel Foods (makers of SPAM), Cheryl Spangler at Giurlani USA (makers of Star Olive Oil), Edward Lowe (founder of Golden Cat Corporation), Peter G. Trybula at Golden Cat Corporation (makers of Tidy Cat), Aura Piedra at Chesebrough-Pond's (makers of Vaseline petroleum jelly), Emmet Burns and Laura Scotiel at Lea & Perrins (makers of Worcestershire Sauce), Paige M. Perdue at the WD-40 Company, Joseph J. Bonk and Lauren Cislak at DowBrands (makers of Ziploc storage bags), Danielle Frizzi at the Gillette Company (makers of Liquid Paper), and Barbara Gargiulo at Tambrands (makers of Tampax tampons).

Upstanding American consumers who shared their pearls of wisdom include Barbara Green, Robert Green, Dr. Jeffrey Gorodetsky, Leonard Sherman, Andrea Brum, Mindy Staley, John Fiore Pucci, Gretchen Van Pelt, Jeffrey Combs, Bill Aitchison, and Dr. Richard Swatt.

Above all, all my love to Debbie and Ashley.

The Fine Print

Sources

■ *All-New Hints from Heloise* by Heloise (New York: Perigee, 1989)

■ *Another Use For* by Vicki Lansky (Deephaven, MN: Book Peddlers, 1991)

■ *Can You Trust a Tomato in January?* by Vince Staten (New York: Simon & Schuster, 1993)

■ *Chicken Soup & Other Folk Remedies* by Joan Wilen and Lydia Wilen (New York: Fawcett Columbine, 1984)

■ *Coca-Cola: An Illustrated History* by Pat Watters (New York: Doubleday, 1978)

■ *Dictionary of Trade Name Origins* by Adrian Room (London: Routledge & Kegan Paul, 1982)

■ *Encyclopedia of Pop Culture* by Jane & Michael Stern (New York: HarperCollins, 1992)

■ "Have a Problem? Chances Are Vinegar Can Help Solve It" by Caleb Solomon (*Wall Street Journal*, September 30, 1992)

■ *Hints from Heloise* by Heloise (New York: Arbor House, 1980)

■ *Hoover's Handbook of World Business 1993* (Austin: Reference Press, 1993)

■ *Hoover's Handbook of American Business 1994* (Austin: Reference Press, 1994)

■ *Household Hints and Handy Tips* by Reader's Digest (Pleasantville, NY: Reader's Digest Association, 1988)

■ *How the Cadillac Got Its Fins* by Jack Mingo (New York: HarperCollins, 1994)

■ *How to Work Wonders with the Wonder Jelly* (Trumbull, CT: Chesebrough-Pond's USA)

■ "Is There Anything Vinegar Is Not Good For?" by Lora Rader (*Country Stock & Small Stock Journal*, March-April 1993)

■ *Kitchen Medicines* by Ben Charles Harris (Barre, MA: Barre, 1968)

■ *Make It Yourself* by Dolores Riccio and Joan Bingham (Radnor, PA: Chilton, 1978)

■ *Mary Ellen's Best of Helpful Hints* by Mary Ellen Pinkham (New York: Warner/B. Lansky, 1979)

■ *Mary Ellen's Greatest Hints* by Mary Ellen Pinkham (New York: Fawcett Crest, 1990)

■ "More Than You Want to Know About SPAM" by Judith Stone (*New York Times Magazine*, July 3, 1994)

■ "A Most Favored Food" by Alice M. Geffen and Carole Berglie (*Americana*, May-June 1989)

■ *The New Our Bodies, Ourselves* by The Boston Women's Health Book Collective (New York: Touchstone, 1992)

■ *Panati's Extraordinary Origins of Everyday Things* by Charles Panati (New York: HarperCollins, 1987)

■ "WD-40," (*USA Today*, 1993)

■ *A Whole Houseful of Uses for Heinz Vinegar* (Pittsburgh, PA: H. J. Heinz, 1993)

■ *Why Did They Name It . . . ?* by Hannah Campbell (New York: Fleet, 1964)

■ *The Woman's Day Help Book* by Geraldine Rhoads and Edna Paradis (New York: Viking, 1988)

Trademark Information

"Bounce" is a registered trademark of Procter & Gamble.

"Clairol" and "Herbal Essences" are registered trademarks of Clairol.

"Coca-Cola" and "Coke" are registered trademarks of the Coca-Cola Company.

"Colgate" is a registered trademark of Colgate-Palmolive.

"Dannon" is a registered trademark of the Dannon Company.

"Efferdent" is a registered trademark of Warner-Lambert.

"Elmer's Glue-All" and Elmer the Bull are registered trademarks of Borden.

"Geritol" is a registered trademark of Beecham, Inc.

"Heinz" is a registered trademark of H. J. Heinz Co.

"Ivory" is a registered trademark of Procter & Gamble.

"Jif" is a registered trademark of Procter & Gamble.

"Kingsford" is a registered trademark of Kingsford Products Company.

"L'eggs" and "Sheer Energy" are registered trademarks of Hanes.

"Listerine" is a registered trademark of Warner-Lambert.

"Maybelline" is a registered trademark of Maybelline.

"Mr. Coffee" is a registered trademark of Mr. Coffee, Inc.

"Morton" and the Morton Umbrella Girl are registered trademarks of Morton International, Inc.

"Nestea" is a registered trademark of Nestlé.

"Quaker Oats" is a registered trademark of the Quaker Oats Company.

"ReaLemon" is a registered trademark of Borden.

"Reynolds Wrap" is a registered trademark of Reynolds Metals.

"Silly Putty" is a registered trademark of Binney & Smith Inc.

"SPAM" and "SPAMBURGER" are registered trademarks of Hormel Foods Corporation.

"Star" is a registered trademark of Giurlani USA.

"Tidy Cat" and "Kitty Litter" are registered trademarks of the Golden Cat Corporation.

"Vaseline" is a registered trademark of Chesebrough-Pond's.

"WD-40" is a registered trademark of the WD-40 Company.

"Worcestershire Sauce" is a registered trademark of Lea & Perrins.
"Ziploc" is a registered trademark of DowBrands L.P.
"Dawn" is a registered trademark of Procter & Gamble.
"Liquid Paper" is a registered trademark of Liquid Paper Corporation.
"Pampers" is a registered trademark of Procter & Gamble.
"Tampax" is a registered trademark of Tambrands Inc.

Index

Acne
Colgate, 14
Listerine, 60
Air freshener
Bounce, 1
Heinz Vinegar, 36
Nestea, 77
Antacid
Heinz Vinegar, 35
Ants, repellent
Heinz Vinegar, 38
Arthritis
Heinz Vinegar, 34
Automobile
air freshener, Bounce, 2
axle grease, Jif, 47
bumpers, Coca-Cola, 9; Reynolds Wrap, 88
dead insects, WD-40, 116
hubcaps, Efferdent, 24
oil, Tidy Cat, 105
seats, dirt, Silly Putty, 93
traction, Tidy Cat, 105
transmission fluid, Tidy Cat, 105
wash, Clairol Herbal Essences, 5
windshield, Maybelline Crystal Clear Nail Polish, 64
Azaleas
Heinz Vinegar, 34

Baked-on food
Bounce, 2
WD-40, 117
Barbecue grill
Reynolds Wrap, 90
Tidy Cat, 106
WD-40, 117

Bathing
L'eggs Sheer Energy, 56
Bathroom fixtures, cleaning
Heinz Vinegar, 35
Bathtub
cleaning, L'eggs Sheer Energy, 57
mildew, Tidy Cat, 105
Battery-operated toys or appliances
Reynolds Wrap, 88
Belt buckles
Maybelline Crystal Clear Nail Polish, 64
Bicycles
WD-40, 116
Blackheads
ReaLemon, 84
Bleeding, heavy
Pampers, 130
Tampax, 130
Bottles, washing
L'eggs Sheer Energy, 56
Brass
ReaLemon, 86
Worcestershire Sauce, 120
Brushes and combs
Clairol Herbal Essences, 6
Bubble bath
Clairol Herbal Essences, 5
Ivory soap, 44
Bubblegum
Jif, 47
Vaseline, 109
WD-40, 116
Bumper stickers, remove
Heinz Vinegar, 38
Bursitis
Star Olive Oil, 102

About the Author

Joey Green was a contributing editor to *National Lampoon* until he wrote an article in *Rolling Stone* on why *National Lampoon* isn't funny anymore. A native of Miami (where he was awarded the *Miami Herald* Silver Knight), Green was almost expelled from Cornell University for selling fake football programs at the 1979 Cornell-Yale homecoming game. He was editor of the *Cornell Lunatic*, president of the National Association of College Humor Magazines, and has authored several books, including *Hellbent on Insanity* (with Bruce Handy and Alan Corcoran), *The Unofficial Gilligan's Island Handbook*, *The Get Smart Handbook*, and *The Partridge Family Album*. Green worked at J. Walter Thompson in New York and Hong Kong, where he wrote television commercials for Burger King, created the launch campaign for the Grand Hyatt Hotel, and won a Clio for a print advertisement he created for Eastman Kodak. He spent two years backpacking around the world on his honeymoon, wrote television commercials for Walt Disney World in Florida, and currently lives in Los Angeles with his wife, Debbie, and their daughter, Ashley.